TRANSFORMING HATE
TO LOVE

This book deserves a prominent place in the public debate about law and order. Indeed, it questions whether the whole issue of emotional disturbance in childhood and adolescence should continue to be regarded as an issue of law and order, or as one requiring a new psychosocial, educational approach. I wish it the widest possible readership.

Marie Jahoda, *Professor Emeritus, University of Sussex*

The Peper Harow residential community was founded in 1970 and gained international repute for its work with disturbed adolescents. For over twenty years this remarkable establishment provided a therapeutic environment for teenagers who had often suffered appalling abuse, and yet for whom the state's remedial provision until then had been in the punitive form of approved schools.

In *Transforming Hate to Love*, Melvyn Rose describes how Peper Harow managed rather than punished disruptive behaviour. Through the words of ex-residents the reader is given a unique view of the effectiveness of the treatment process – its successes and its failures.

The overwhelmingly positive outcome of Rose's interviews with ex-residents of Peper Harow indicates that the predominantly punitive bias of current social policy in this area reflects an incomplete view of the causes of criminality among young people. Peper Harow's success demonstrates to both the general and specialist reader how a psychodynamic approach to adolescent disturbance and delinquency, and its emotional source, could benefit society as a whole.

Melvyn Rose was the founder director of Peper Harow and its director for thirteen years. He went on to found the Peper Harow Foundation, leaving in 1993 to pursue a career as a writer and consultant.

TRANSFORMING HATE TO LOVE

An outcome study of the Peper Harow
treatment process for adolescents

Melvyn Rose

London and New York

First published 1997
by Routledge
11 New Fetter Lane, London EC4P 4EE

Simultaneously published in the USA and Canada
by Routledge
29 West 35th Street, New York, NY 10001

Typeset in Bembo and Trade Gothic by M Rules
Printed and bound in Great Britain by
TJ International Ltd, Padstow, Cornwall

British Library Cataloguing in Publication Data
A catalogue record for this book is available from the British Library.

Library of Congress Cataloguing in Publication Data
Rose, Melvyn
    Transforming hate to love ... an outcome study of the Peper
Harow treatment process for adolescents / Melvyn Rose
        p.   cm.
    Includes bibliographical references and index.
    ISBN 0-415-13831-0 (hc). — ISBN 0-415-13832-9 (pbk.)
    1. Peper Harow (Institution) 2. Adolescent psychotherapy
Residential treatment England Case studies. 3. Therapeutic
communities England Case studies. I. Title.
RJ504.5.R673   1997
616.89′14′0835—dc21   96-46581
                                                        CIP

ISBN 0-415-13831-0 (hbk)
ISBN 0-415-13832-9 (pbk)

CONTENTS

FOREWORD

In 1970 Melvyn Rose began to change Peper Harow, then an Approved School of which he was a staff member, into a therapeutic community to whose direction he devoted the next thirteen years. He was supported by a Board of Trustees and by mainly new staff members who shared his conviction that the application of the insights achieved by psychodynamic psychology were a better guide for the treatment of disturbed youngsters than the dominant public policies. These were more designed to appease an anxious public and to fulfil the desire for revenge of the victims of juvenile misdeeds than to help the young to change their way of life. Rose has fully described the ideas and procedures guiding the management of the therapeutic community in a previous book (Rose 1990).

The present book is the account of a type of study which is all too rarely undertaken, though it deals with the most crucial question that needs to be asked about any therapy: What is the lasting outcome?

Strictly speaking, a complete answer to this question requires a comparison with the effects of other treatments, both in terms of the psychological outcome and its financial costs. Accordingly the original plan for Rose's study included such comparison. To run a therapeutic community is certainly not cheap. It requires highly trained staff and a high staff/resident ratio. It is also important that the young people live in a residence that would wordlessly help to kindle their undermined self-esteem. At 1983 prices, a year at Peper Harow cost approximately £21,000 per resident. This covered all programme costs including some regular material maintenance costs, but no capital costs which were fund-raised. Inquiries from relevant institutions revealed the amazing and deplorable absence, at least in the public domain, of comparable data about any other form of treatment of youngsters in trouble – not for the 'short, sharp shock', not for Borstals, not for remand or any other form of detention, nor for fostering or any other form of residential care. However, informed opinion holds that if to the running costs of other treatments, capital and central administrative costs were added, as well as the costs of dealing with the apparent recidivism of young offenders and the mental and social breakdown of others, a therapeutic community might emerge as relatively cheap.

What cannot be expressed in pounds is the psychological impact of Peper Harow as summarised in Table 1 (p. 58). This is indeed dramatic.

Ten to twenty-five years after leaving Peper Harow, the vast majority of the sample of ex-residents lead useful responsible lives, though prior to Peper Harow they seemed destined for prison, mental institutions or suicide. These results are so gratifying that they may arouse suspicion in the reader that only successful cases had been included in the sample. The study methods are fully described in Chapter 7. Here it must suffice to say, so as to forestall such suspicions, that a strictly random selection of cases was performed.

One element of selection operated however. For psychological reasons fully explained in Chapter 2, to become a resident at Peper Harow an element of self-selection existed. While the local councils tended to refer their most intractable cases for the intake interview, which was confirmed by independent, reputable research in the 1970s (Millham, Bullock and Hosie 1978), Peper Harow's interview objective was to initiate a youngster's engagement with a new psychotherapeutic way of dealing with his or her problems. Following the offer of a place by Peper Harow, applicants were only admitted if they wrote a letter in which they personally and voluntarily committed themselves. During Rose's directorship, almost no applicants refused to do so.

At a time when a not inconsiderable portion of the young generation is demoralised, without hope for their future, without faith and ideals, playing truant from school and life, then the old and weak have learned, with reason, to fear the young, and not only in inner cities.

This book deserves a prominent place in the public debate about law and order. Indeed, it questions whether the whole issue of emotional disturbance in childhood and adolescence should continue to be regarded as an issue of law and order, or as one requiring a new psychosocial, educational approach. I wish it the widest possible readership.

Marie Jahoda
April 1996

ACKNOWLEDGEMENTS

I cannot sufficiently express my thanks to Professor Emeritus Marie Jahoda, of Sussex University. She taught and encouraged me through many hours of consultation, both in preparation for and during the course of this study. Her learned attention would improve any such endeavour, but her patience and humanity and her exceptional ability to clarify makes her tuition one of life's memorable experiences.

Nor would anything but the most fulsome appreciation be appropriate for the ex-residents of Peper Harow who bravely participated in this venture and also for the many ex-residents who, though not part of the research study, knew of its general objectives and who were equally enthusiastic and encouraging.

I am, not for the first time, extremely grateful to The Tudor Trust for its trustees' and staff's enthusiastic interest in the struggles of young people to overcome adversity. The Trust's financial support made a serious study possible, while its continuous contribution to the Steering Committee added a necessary critical overview.

Mrs Judith Arbow, as the professional researcher, worked indefatigably in the early part of the project. Her sensitive interviewing and meticulous administrative skills were critical to the whole endeavour, while her informed advice since has made her participation especially valued.

The trustees of The Peper Harow Foundation and staff, especially Mrs Monica Hutchinson, generously enabled the many carefully preserved documents pertaining to the study to be researched and analysed. Without their enthusiasm for the project's objectives, this would have been a far less accurate book.

My appreciation is also offered to John Rae-Price and the staff of the National Children's Bureau, who administered the research grant, and to Barbara Kahan and to Dr Michael Little of The Dartington Social Research Unit, for their advice and for pointing me in the direction of important relevant research material. I am also very grateful for the patience and advice given by Dr Earl Hopper, President of The International Association of Group Psychoanalysis and by Dr William Barnes-Gutteridge of the University of Stirling, both of whom examined later versions of the text from their respective and valued particular professional insights.

Finally, I must thank my family for their tolerance and patience during this all-consuming and lengthy gestation. Thanks are particularly due to my wife, Dr Susan E. Rose, for drawing various paediatric and other medical texts to my attention and also for her patient and diplomatic criticism, having been inveigled into reading endless drafts and, despite all, for her essential encouragement throughout.

As with any such work, there are always many people who have contributed, sometimes unwittingly, in the form of their own work perhaps, or of their own example. Each unique influence has helped me to recognise the creativity of young residents at Peper Harow and of their deeply caring staff.

1

INTRODUCTION

Most of the youngsters at Peper Harow had either experienced serious abuse in their early life, or had not been given enough emotional nourishment for normal psychological development. Lacking the personality strengths appropriate for adolescents, they frequently regarded other people and the environment around themselves in a way very different from that of most young people of their age. They would, for instance, feel persecuted by minor adversities, or would regard their own hostility and abusiveness towards others as merely trivial, or even in some perverse way as appropriate! They diced with seriously destructive lifestyles, or activities such as drugs or prostitution, all of which behaviour had derived from their malfunctioning personalities. Unless they could be helped to see themselves and the world around them more realistically and unless they could develop the strengths needed to cope with that reality, their future prospects seemed inevitably catastrophic. They would be unable to sustain adult intimate relationships, or worse, they would become increasingly violent or criminal, or they would suffer a steady deterioration in their mental health, or become alcoholics or drug addicts. They would suffer and cause suffering to others and would be likely to become a permanent burden on the resources of society. This was Peper Harow's challenge then – to what extent could it develop a residential programme that would enable its residents to gain a more normal lifestyle instead? This, of course, had been the objective of many other institutions – Approved Schools and Borstals, Maladjusted Schools and Adolescent Units – but the success of those institutions had been worryingly inadequate, despite considerable organisational and financial investment.

So much fear was ingrained at the root of the Peper Harow residents' beings that the emotional energy normally devoted to growth and creativity had instead to be spent in 'keeping the lid on'. This emotional foreclosure was actually a compulsive defence against the reality of their

1

painful life experiences. The youngsters, without being consciously aware of it, felt themselves compelled to deny how terrible they fantasised themselves as being. It was as though to acknowledge such unconscious feelings would somehow confirm that they truly were that monstrously bad and dangerous and that, if this were so, they would indeed deserve nothing but punishment and suffering. At the least, they would not be entitled even to hope for normal relationships.

Peper Harow was itself a most disturbing experience for such young people, because it deliberately set out to counter their self-destructive, compulsive defences by offering them the best environment it could muster and the best adult commitment which the staff as a group could create. All of this social, intellectual and emotional nurture was paradoxically frightening and threatening, because until then many youngsters had become emotionally numbed by their continual adverse experience. They had few positive expectations from others, or from themselves, whereas at Peper Harow the most enormous expectations both attracted and challenged them and these were presented in forms that could not easily be resisted.

Few ordinary people understand how terrible life is for such youngsters. Everyone is clear when they produce behaviour that is terrible for other people – especially when their teachers, the passers-by in the local shopping mall, or homeowners with years of hopes and hard work tied up in their possessions, are abused or frightened or robbed by aggressive teenagers. And it is absolutely right that no one's personal injuries should give them the right to hurt others. It is also true that even human beings who have experienced the most fortunate upbringing and education are still so often selfish that we actually need a structure of law and of social values to help us keep our exploitativeness of others and of our environment within bounds. For most of us, it can be argued that punishment for our transgressions does have a salutary effect. Perhaps most of us are deterred from wrongdoing, as much because of our fear of the consequences as because of our own moral beliefs and self-respect.

But the youngsters at Peper Harow were exceptions to this. For all the qualitatively varied discussions about deviant behaviour and crime that take place constantly in our rapidly changing society, the differences between those for whom sanctions are effective and those whose transgressions are worsened by punishment are almost never made clear. Right and wrong does matter to most people. Our experience of being considerate towards others in turn results in a positive response towards us. For most of us, this expectation was germinated by the exchange of our very first loving smiles in infancy. However, if instead of smiles and instead of tender sensitivity to the infant's vulnerability and towards his or her as yet undeveloped ability to make sense of their environment, a baby had been beaten or screamed at or worse, he or she would not thereafter be spontaneously on the look-out for the opportunity to please others in order to attract their positive attention in return. Instead, he or she would be rendered constantly anxious and would even resist the very nurture that was so vitally needed, being unsure about what might also accompany it. Therefore, real food itself might often be angrily rejected. Forcing a parent to wait endlessly for a positive response can be a potent weapon for a baby. But would such anxious anger encourage his or her parents' sensitive determination to understand what is upsetting their baby, or would they instead respond to the baby's knocking a plate to the floor, for instance, by 'teaching him a lesson that he will never forget'?

As far as disturbed teenagers are concerned, a punitive response to their inappropriate behaviour may be a significant further step down the road to catastrophe. It certainly will not make things better! Nevertheless, the purpose of all the attention and nurture and tolerance at Peper Harow was not, as some of our envious neighbours felt, to reward the undeserving and to make a mockery of justice. Its sole object was to reconstruct, or often to construct for the first time, the emotional, intellectual and social conditions that are the foundation of a normal personality. If this process were to be successful, it would not mean that the young person would thereafter be reborn as an angel. At best, he or she would have been set free to become an adult among other adults, capable of developing and sustaining a moral base to his or her life, capable of germinating positive goals and capable of generating the sustained effort necessary for bringing these aims to fruition. But it would also inevitably mean that, like most adults, he or she would also fall short of their ideals and would sometimes feel inadequate and unable to identify with the self-image that they would most like. In other words, they would have been given the key to adulthood – albeit problematically later in their lives than is normal – but they would only have been liberated to make what they could of it, for better or worse. Peper Harow's success would have been in restoring to them the birthright to which all youngsters should feel entitled.

However, starting from where they did, even limited goals would often seem as unattainable as Everest! And yet the youngsters themselves frequently spoke of their hopes of being 'sorted out' – as though this would free them from any problems and enable them to achieve their most desired aspirations. What is more, they often assumed that staff must have attained just such perfection, or otherwise what 'know-how' could they possibly have to impart? Perhaps such naive over-idealisation of the staff and of their own anticipated rewards arose from several sources, which in fact tell us something about the mental contortions people seem to need to put themselves through in order to risk an attempt to change the way they are. Unless they could encourage themselves sufficiently with the fabulous temptations of success, they would fear never being able to make a sufficient leap of faith and imagination to trigger 'lift-off' on their therapeutic journey. Sometimes the staff did not altogether discourage such unreality. The youngsters' unexpected willingness to consider what the staff were offering often came as a surprising relief from their unremitting resistance. Often the youngsters felt that unless they could almost deify staff in their minds, it would be impossible to believe that relationships with them would be any different from their past experiences of adults. But, simultaneously, the youngster's compulsive ability to deny truth and even reality could exhaust the most committed adult.

Because of this sometimes collusively unrealistic perception of a successful outcome, idealised 'success' at Peper Harow was typified in fantasy as someone who was leaving to go to university, who was evidently creative, astoundingly patient and kind to others, with exceptionally righteous standards of honesty and personal behaviour – in other words, a paragon of all the virtues and abilities! Although one or two ex-residents do seem to have developed remarkable personal qualities, it is hardly surprising that most of them are no better or worse than the rest of society. Moreover, such unreality at Peper Harow sometimes concealed other people's achievements, although from their individual starting situation these might have been equally remarkable. Among those interviewed for this study were a high proportion who left Peper Harow under a cloud. They either were asked to leave and were regarded as failures, or they stomped out in high dudgeon. Many are still bitter about this and believe that their life would have turned out to be radically better if they had achieved more at Peper Harow. In fact, almost without exception, they acknowledge that such experience as they were able to take with them has had an infinitely worthwhile effect on their life since. What has frequently astonished those who were staff at Peper Harow has been how well even so-called failures have turned out. It may have taken them some years of struggle beyond their residential experience to attain a realistic sense of who they are and of what they want in life. However, what they repeatedly say is that it was the actual experiences with which they did engage at Peper Harow that have sustained their struggle towards later achievements and self-respect.

In *Healing Hurt Minds* (Rose 1990), the author set out to write a purely subjective description of how the healing programme was developed at Peper Harow. But however anecdotally interesting this might be, it demonstrates the need for an additional opinion of the treatment process – one that derives from the ex-residents' views of their experience. Has the youngster's experience there really had anything to do with the way they say they are living today – as many as twenty-five years later? The ex-residents' views about the relative worth of one aspect or another of their experience inevitably vary, not just according to the level of their emotional capacity to recognise and engage with different forms of nurture, but also according to how well-developed the resources actually were at the specific time they were at Peper Harow. Several ex-residents from the earliest days describe experiences that would definitely not have made for security. Others describe visiting after some years, to find that the physical and material environment had developed to a standard that made them realise how much they themselves had missed.

And then, of course, those of us responsible for the venture were inevitably more limited in skill and insight when we began. Our own calibre and maturity also varied. Was the practice we did effect really good enough and, where it was inadequate, could it have been put right had we known what we know now? Even with the wisdom of hindsight, there may still be intractable emotional conditions for which we do not yet have an effective response. For instance, although Bowlby's work after the end of the Second World War left one in no doubt as to the serious psychological consequences of deprivation (Bowlby 1966), the extent and seriousness of child sexual abuse has only been widely recognised comparatively recently. Had we been more alive to that issue in the earliest days of Peper Harow, it is probable that addressing its consequences would have boosted our understanding of the significance of all our relationships within the Community, with the result that there would have been more effective help.

Goffman and others had by 1970 already defined the further injury that is caused to vulnerable people by the tendencies of closed institutions to depersonalise individuals (Goffman 1968). Those who saw their institutions as therapeutic communities assumed that they were expressing a culture and style that would counter such dangers. Several of us at Peper Harow had previous experience of institutionalising establishments. Thus we would have been quite shocked if we had realised how difficult it was going to be to avoid our own programmes developing a similar depersonalising effect, especially when our permissive and democratic style was supposed to be so libertarian! Yet we still pressurised residents to be compliant and to accept, without too much question, the authority of the hierarchy. After all, the hierarchy saw itself as being 'on the side of the residents'! Yet if liberty had not been regarded predominantly as the freedom to co-operate, could the Community have existed at all? It was a problem that the 1969 Children and Young Persons' Act had set out to address, that is – how to meet the needs of children and adolescents in a way that can manage their behaviour yet still restore their potential future lives. Twenty years on, the government was still trying to effect legislation (The Children Act 1989) that would bring this about! However, some of the consequences of this well-intentioned legislation and its associated governmental reports and guidelines, have actually been to inhibit rather than to enhance the therapeutic endeavours of residential centres.

It is obviously unacceptable that institutions specifically established to care for young people should abuse them in any way. Several notorious cases in recent years have demonstrated how especially vulnerable such children are.

> It is a common belief that only 'bad' agencies and only 'sick' people are involved in residential abuse. The reality is that even those agencies with exceptional risk management policies are not free from the possibility of employing a high-risk person.
>
> (Bloom 1993: 91–92)

However, the treatment process, especially with disturbed adolescents, can be damaged by inadequate insight and unmanaged attitudes and behaviour that may not be legally, or even consciously abusive.

> Treating youngsters who are moderately to severely psychiatrically disordered in institutional settings often arouses in staff intense sexual feelings. 'Erotic' rather than 'sexual' is the preferred term . . . to indicate that although some of these reactions are, in the final analysis, indeed sexual in nature, the way they are manifested usually assumes many deceptive forms . . . such as 'too much hugging', 'too much "spoiling"', or to use a currently favored term – too much 'bonding'.
>
> (Ponce 1993: 107)

Such behaviour becomes abusive when it adds to youngsters' existing confusion or misunderstanding. To a young person who has been seriously abused, a hug may not mean the same as it would to a child in a well-functioning family. Instead, it may feel like the first step that will end in frank abuse. Thus the young person's fragile trust of the adult may freeze at the very moment where his or her real need is for it to take root and grow. The consequences could even be the essential failure of the programme for that youngster.

The specific emotional needs of young people in residential settings are complex and varied, and both the Children Act 1989 and its sequential guidelines, *The Care of Children 1990*, attempt not only to protect children, but to ensure that their needs and their individual rights as children are both properly met. Sometimes these conflict. For instance, in order to ensure the absence of abuse and also that all protective legislation, including health and safety legislation, is being met there can be as many as twenty inspections of a small children's home in the same month. It is very difficult to enable children to feel that they share the ownership of their home and its process when so many strangers are allowed access without regard to the feelings of the children or staff. Attempts to ensure the protection of a youngster's sense of individuality may produce policies – for instance, that all children should have their own room, or be supervised by a night shift of waking staff – without any reference to their psychological needs which may be completely different for one youngster than for another.

What tend to be overlooked and certainly not understood are the psychological needs of children in care. A recent survey of all the children in the care of the County of Essex, for example, found that almost all of them required some kind of psychological help (Bunce 1994). Unfortunately, in local authorities the focus cannot simply be upon understanding and meeting the complex needs of the child in care. It also has financial obligations and various responsibilities towards its electorate as well as towards other groups with special needs, and in addition has to follow the requirements of central government.

In Kahan's recent and comprehensive description of the needs of children in homes, she emphasises that

> Residential care staff will be closest to and in touch with the whole child and his world and, in consequence, will be key figures in co-ordinating the work of other professionals.
>
> (Kahan 1994: 115)

But the hierarchical relationships in large local authority organisations act against this. Financial exigencies may well determine the institutionalisation of furnishing. Fire regulations may well produce warning systems that are geared to public institutions rather than a private home. The health and safety regulations about the environment and use of kitchens can seriously impede the interpersonal experience deriving from the cooking and eating of food that children brought up in institutions so desperately need. As always, the issue of financial resources effects both the kind of staff who can be recruited and the calibre of essential staff-support systems. Kahan specifically emphasises the different but mutually related and equally essential systems for the training, support, development and professional supervision of staff working with emotionally disturbed children and young people (*ibid.*: 255–274). Ensuring that staff have time to engage in such ongoing professional programmes also raises costs, as does providing high-calibre professionals to effect them. Were a local authority to ensure this quality of staff resource within a series of small children's homes, the cost would inevitably be greater per capita than in a large institution. Meanwhile, local authorities' objectives are inevitably more concerned to reconcile the conflicting priorities of more needs than can be paid for than to focus entirely on the psychodynamic of their staff and children in each of their homes. It is extremely difficult for the systems of control required of officers by the elected representatives not to be mechanistic instead of sensitive to the need for emotional nurture of staff and very difficult children.

Lacking confidence in the outcome of the 1969 Children and Young Persons' Act, Peper Harow deliberately set out to manage a psychotherapeutic process independently, but soon itself faced similar contradictions between the exigent managerial requirements of an organisational entity and the complex needs of the youngsters themselves. In trying to reconcile these it became impossible, especially at the beginning, for the practice at Peper Harow to be good other than in parts. Fundamental problems also arise from the nature of the therapeutic process itself. And indeed, any kind of programme with disturbed youngsters has its own set of problems to overcome. For example, some adolescents need a strong institution to wrestle with. If their need for aggressive rebellion is greater than normal, then so must be the strength of a community if it is to tolerate and contain the youngsters' aggression more successfully than the family groups within which the seeds of their excessive hostility have been engendered. However, while determining to demonstrate to one youngster that it is safe for them to be containable and that any limitations to their personal freedom will not actually destroy them, despite the traumatic lessons of their past lives, another youngster's anxiety in response to group pressure will cause him or her to capitulate compliantly once again rather than to co-operate appropriately. There is much evidence to demonstrate that it is the compulsively compliant who are most vulnerable to sexual abuse. Obviously then, balancing the functioning of communal life so as to do the maximum therapeutic good and no serious harm, demands a highly sophisticated programme. Perhaps our main advantage, as an independent charitable organisation, lay in our ability to respond quickly and directly to perceived need. The director of the programme, for instance, rather than the local authority's director of finance, albeit with proper safeguards, could make financial decisions that acknowledged the priority of the youngsters' needs.

The design of this programme at Peper Harow assumed that the Community was a kaleidoscope of interactions between groups and individuals at different levels of group and individual consciousness. It tried to be diagnostically sensitive to the psychological significance of the Community's everyday life for each of its residents. Special efforts were made to anticipate what any individual might feel in response to an argument in the Community Meeting for instance. This in turn might determine which member of staff would simply sit next to that individual or whether, instead, a member of staff might set time aside to talk after the meeting about some of that youngster's feelings, or perhaps the member of staff might encourage other youngsters to take the individual off to the music room, or to play a game down by the river. The simplest of interventions can be as profoundly therapeutic as an intensive hour's psychoanalytic psychotherapy, provided its timing is well judged and the person making the intervention actually recognises its emotional significance to the recipient.

Thus, a residential treatment programme is a complex amalgam of many ingredients, implying many things about the training and supervision of staff. Its very complexity should emphasise the difficulty for an agency with a managerial responsibility to ensure that a particular lifestyle and culture occurs with an individual institution. Developing the direct management skill within the particular institution to ensure the development and maintenance of a therapeutic culture is itself a complex ongoing task. The temptation of local or central government is to issue guidelines to try to ensure that children are not abused. However, defensively prioritising protection may well result in the serious emotional needs of the majority of children in residence being neglected, which is why so many continue to break down on leaving care. In fact, children are far more likely to be safe when they are actually part of an effective treatment programme and when they have a sense that their most inexpressible needs are nevertheless understood.

Working with children and adolescents often enriches the professional through the parenting opportunities it provides. Human qualities of sensitivity and tenderness are called up from within us in response to the youngsters' underlying need and suffering. Fred Lenhoff of Shotton Hall School, when asked about in-service training and development, often used to say, 'The one thing we are doing here is preparing our young staff to become exceptional parents'! Again and again at Peper Harow, the importance of an individual member of staff's commitment and care seems to have been the catalyst for the resident's personal commitment towards change. And to convince a desperately defensive youngster to lower his or her guard against an adult's caring – despite the youngster's conviction that this could only mean further pain and disappointment – certainly requires more than even the most highly skilled technical know-how. Though Bettelheim was undoubtedly correct that *Love Is Not Enough* (Bettelheim 1965), without it, intellectual understanding and knowledge are not enough either.

However, one of the most difficult problems to manage in the residential setting is the inevitable closeness of the staff's and of the youngsters' interpersonal emotional involvement. Relationships often seem to be as close as in a family, yet these feelings have arisen suddenly and without the concomitant growth of familial taboos that structure and thus manage the boundaries of intimacy and intensity of feeling between the sexes and between the generations. Many institutions are so daunted by the task of trying to manage these frequently exposed feelings that they try to place defensive embargoes on their expression. And yet in a Community whose main purpose is to illuminate the significance of the residents' functioning, should behaviour really be driven out of sight? Instead, self-awareness and insight need to be sufficiently developed to be able to contain inappropriate behaviour and to promote an emotionally nourishing environment. This too has considerable implications for resources, for training and selection, for clinical supervision and for organisational objectives that ideally would be fully understood and agreed by referring agencies and the wider Community.

Therapeutic communities in fact exist within a society which has contradictory standards of behaviour and with fundamental attitudes and values that are often exploitative. Society often expresses these contradictions pruriently and by scapegoating. So the management within such a community of the residents' interpersonal, disturbed behaviour is bound to be pressured by public opinion, whether or not this is informed by an awareness of the needs of emotionally injured children.

Sharon, one of the contributors to this book, had been sexually abused by her father very seriously and over many years. The outcome was that the father went to prison, the family broke up, other siblings blamed the whistle-blower and she was left to carry all the guilt for the huge amount of damage that could in no way be regarded as her responsibility. There are many issues that underlie the inflexible way that sexual abuse, or the suspicion of it, is sometimes handled. Occasionally, it seems that the desire to blame and punish is what is pre-eminent, rather than the necessary concern for the psychological welfare of the abused youngster.

Functioning within a society that is ambivalent about its concern for those with difficult behaviour and about its own values, it is very hard for staff to focus objectively on the meaning of disturbed children's behaviour. It is very hard not to be over-influenced by ill-informed and judgmental outside pressures. The task may actually be to help the youngsters understand themselves in sufficient depth to begin to feel and behave differently, but the pressure to restrain behaviour sometimes hinders the growth of insight. It is also difficult for the press not to publicise, with outraged righteousness, the inadequacies of residential establishments which have seriously failed in their task of care.

The greater problem by far for the management of a residential treatment centre is to ensure the proper functioning of the unconscious dynamic processes. Well managed, the existence of these processes can ensure that the residential placement engenders a truly new life prospect for an emotionally disturbed youngster, though how difficult it is to guarantee the consistent quality of such a programme cannot be sufficiently stressed. For a start, because the residential community is distanced from everyday life, its normal social inhibitions are lowered, while the stress on the group from the greater incidence of acted-out feelings is raised. The enactment of such feelings makes the boundaries which normally limit other people's fantasies feel more fragile. This insecurity promotes a desire for rules and punishments rather than for more patience and more group responsibility. It is easier to become judgmental and moralistically defensive rather than insightful and self-aware.

The ultimate job of the staff is, in various ways, to hold the ring on all the emotional turmoil and to ensure that everyday life in the community feels growthful rather than disintegrative. This promotes just sufficient security to enable youngsters to express and to receive kindness and perceptivity. However, it is much easier to blame and condemn. Nevertheless, if the adults are to be effective, then it is especially inappropriate for staff to climb onto moralistic perches in order to pontificate about behaviour. Instead, among their many kinds of skilled contribution, they need to be exceptionally clear about their own emotional functioning. Such self-awareness will promote a sense of security for the youngsters and, at the same time, offer an example to balance the youngsters' pathological and destructive attitudes.

The therapeutic community is intended to operate as a total system, and sometimes its unconscious group processes may be at odds with its visible structure. For instance, in the daily Community Meeting, the staff as a group may become very defensive should some of their own relationships, for example, be questioned by the youngsters. More damage may be caused by avoiding the enquiry than by a straightforward acknowledgement, even of personal inadequacy. Sometimes staff may fall into the defensive trap of interpreting the enquiry as evidence of the youngster's unhealthy interest, rather than as a legitimate concern about the staff's sense of responsibility. Not surprisingly, avoiding a legitimate concern may generate considerable resentment, as injunctions to 'Do as I say, not as I do' are provocative. But the difference also undermines the youngster's ability to trust the adults. Continual care is needed if the abusive use of insight is to be avoided.

Inevitably, adults too are fallible. At the same time, the actual psycho-dynamic challenges for them of life within a therapeutic community are extraordinary, making their task exceptionally stressful. And yet, for all that, the parent-like staff can still prove to be staunch and nurturing friends to the youngsters. The youngsters' faith in them and in their intelligent insight can help the youngsters find faith in themselves. The staff's patient tolerance can provide a psychically secure emotional environment for the youngster, giving him or her the time they need to recover and grow. The staff's exceptional personalities and talents can provide the truly valued role models that are so important for adolescents. These qualities are almost impossible to provide with sufficient consistency outside the residential establishment. However, even though some institutions have failed to maintain the consistent quality of their programme, to conclude that the residential option should be discarded would be to waste a unique oppor-tunity. An effective quality-assurance system can be designed not only to guarantee that the objectives are being appropriately pursued, but also to do so without undermining staff. It can be both trusting and objective.

As has already been suggested, managing the therapeutic endeavour in such a sophisticated way cannot be achieved *ab initio* and without having to learn from painful mistakes. And even when a community's programme has reached a level of sophistication, there are natural oscillations in its functioning (Savalle and Wagenborg 1980). In other words, trying to pin down an organic process of psychological growth and change, is like trying to ensure that the air we breathe is pure. With a great deal of sci-entific knowledge and personal commitment it can be done – more or less.

In 1970, Peper Harow as an organisation set out to develop a pro-gramme that really would change the lives of the youngsters who went there. The issues that arose after the founding director left in 1983 to establish the Peper Harow Foundation are not for this book. They are in themselves complex. Ultimately, Peper Harow closed in 1993. What the following chapters focus on arises from a study of the ex-residents' views of what happened to them at Peper Harow and since. The details of how the study was conducted and its results can be found in the final chapter.

Many quotations are taken from the transcripts of the lengthy interviews which formed the prime source of the research investigation. Information about the sample of ex-residents largely results from the analysis of these transcripts, but also from the referral papers which are to be found in the ex-residents' confidential files. Therefore, this book is the result of a co-operative venture with the ex-residents. It is shaped by their own undeniably authentic and hopeful voices. Their ongoing struggle is an example of what can be done to transform the most intransigent situation into success.

2

A DESIGN FOR CHANGE
AND GROWTH

The Peper Harow endeavour was a response to increasing recognition that previous disciplinary regimes, such as Approved Schools, had produced little change in those who had been sent there. The youngsters believed that they had been sent for punishment and this directly affected their response. Accordingly, they remained resistant and resentful to the well-intended efforts of even the most enthusiastic adult. Staff ran well-resourced trade-training departments, stimulating mountain and canoe expeditions, demonstrated personal interest in the youngsters through pastoral programmes and psychiatric consultancy, as well as experimenting with activities such as education within the local community. In the best of those institutions, discipline, while strict compared with the peer group lifestyle outside, was generally fair. At first sight, therefore, it was astonishing that the success rate, measured by re-offending and by the numbers remaining employed in the trade for which they had been trained for more than a year, was often less than 20 per cent. Staff were demoralised by such failure and often became cynical and mistrustful of the youngsters. There were institutional systems for rewarding co-operation and progress by the youngsters, though there was no concept that youngsters and adults should share an equal commitment to the institutional objectives. Instead, the general relationships between these two groups were emotionally superficial rather than psychotherapeutic.

The occasional but exceptionally newsworthy examples of abuse within such institutions often encouraged the popular notion that structure and discipline *per se*, were abusive. The spirit of the times certainly made both issues unfashionable. Nevertheless, alternative ideas, such as those of A.S. Neill at Summerhill (Neill 1975), which had been seen as encouraging more liberal and creative lifestyles, rapidly became synonymous in many people's minds with anarchy. Experiments with so-called permissive regimes (Cornish and Clarke 1968) seemed to provide no better results than those

14

of highly disciplined approaches, because neither programme recognised that the ability to function socially and to cope with the variety of relationships in normal life arises neither from the imposition of rules of behaviour, nor from a *laissez-faire* attitude towards child-rearing. Unfortunately, those responsible for managing problem youngsters had little understanding of the complex process of psychological development that underpins even normal behaviour and attitudes towards oneself and others.

The theoretical model that was most helpful to those of us responsible for Peper Harow's metamorphosis from senior Approved School to therapeutic Community was that developed by Erik Erikson (Erikson 1959). He envisages psychological development and social development as a symbiotic process that continues throughout life. As we age, so we fulfil different functions in relation to others, while our self-perspective changes accordingly. Erikson sees the period we call Adolescence as a pivotal one. In physical and also in psychosocial terms, Adolescence is the period of transition from dependent Childhood to independent Adulthood, during which demands for personal commitment in one's psychosocial attitudes and responsibilities steadily increase. This emotional engagement with one's activities and within one's relationships is an essential quality for successful intimacy with a partner and for eventual child-rearing, but it is equally essential in coping with less intimate social relationships such as those within employment.

The psychological ingredients that enable us to manage adult life successfully begin their development at the beginning of Infancy and lead on through periods that Erikson categorises as Early Childhood, Play Age and School Age, through to Adolescence. Each period challenges us with new psychosocial tasks to resolve and, as we do so, each success also enhances our emotional self-confidence and our skill at solving psychological problems. The nurturing effect of our successes strengthens our abilities to manage the developmental tasks of the next period. Adolescence is seen both as a preparative time for Young Adulthood and beyond, as well as being a recapitulative time, when all the experience of the past is reassessed before becoming integrated with the continuously nourishing roots of our personality.

Erikson also paints the gloomier parallel picture, which arises when this growthful sequence is damaged by traumatic or emotionally depriving life experiences. To a varying extent, almost all the youngsters sent to residential establishments had been emotionally deprived or damaged. Although many did not actually need a residential experience in order to put the past right, within others the actual developmental psychological process, including the capacity for recovery, had been very seriously

15

injured. As a result, those youngsters lacked the capacity to use the age-appropriate experiences of everyday life. This sometimes lifelong incapacity made the consequences for their future as adults dire.

When we were establishing Peper Harow as a therapeutic Community, Erikson's theory of normal and abnormal development helped us to clarify what should have happened to our youngsters, as well as shedding light on what kind of damage had been caused by their unpropitious past experiences. In addition, we were enormously helped by George Lyward's therapeutic Community for adolescent boys at Finchden Manor in Kent, which had then operated for more than forty years (Burn 1956). The development of its psychologically nourishing and challenging lifestyle demonstrated how effective psychotherapy in the residential context could be, even for the most injured of young people.

It was very much these exceptionally emotionally damaged youngsters that we set out to help at Peper Harow. There had always been youngsters in residential institutions with sufficiently good psychological experience to overcome their current difficulties, if they received some help. In fact, such partly well-functioning youngsters were being decreasingly referred to residential establishments, as local authorities came to bear the full costs that had previously been shouldered by central government. As we shall see, those who were predominantly replacing them had experienced a variety of exceptionally damaging upbringings, so that without effective treatment all their prognoses – both psychologically and socially – appeared to be disastrous, as were the prognoses for their own children which they were likely to rear within a few years.

The initial question for us at Peper Harow was how to change both the existing Senior Approved School for delinquent boys and the staff – who were also resistant to change – into a place of healing and growth. The Approved School occupied an estate in Surrey owned by a charitable trust. The estate mansion, called Peper Harow, had been built on the site of an earlier great house of the same name whose existence was recorded in the Domesday Book. The existing mansion had been designed by one of England's leading eighteenth-century architects and its uncompromising Palladian style perfectly represented the self-assured superiority of the aristocracy at the height of the Age of Elegance. The surrounding park swept graciously down to the River Wey, providing a panoramic view across the Surrey Commons to the Devil's Punchbowl, nearly ten miles distant. Great cedars of Lebanon and oriental plane trees had been planted to ensure continually intriguing vistas as one strolled. It was astonishingly beautiful and totally different from what those who came to live there would have imagined home to be. Nevertheless, within its totally unfamiliar environment we still set out to engender those normal feelings that gradually amalgamate to form a sense of personal security and worth.

Redl and Wineman, in their classic *Children Who Hate* (Redl and Wineman 1951), personify that part of a disturbed youngster's personality that resists any emotional response, by humorously calling it 'the delinquent ego'. They describe the many twists and turns of such an ego's resistance, in particular, to anything that seems to call for a change of attitude. At one time the delinquent ego is compliant towards adult demands, while actually remaining emotionally unmoved. At another time the delinquent ego is hostile and aggressive, arousing acute anxiety in staff and provoking their rejection. This rejection, then, in turn, becomes used falsely to confirm to the youngsters that adults never really care for children anyway! Redl and Wineman describe this defence against a youngster's willingness to review their general emotional stance as deriving from an acute underlying fear of vulnerability, a legacy of many truly injurious past experiences that had resulted whenever the youngster had actually allowed another person to get close to him or her. In *Children Who Hate*, the authors demonstrate how the task of overcoming resistance to insight and awareness is essential if change is to occur, despite the difficulty in doing so. However, such youngsters are professional resisters and they are so practised in recognising even the hint of a demand for change in attitude and behaviour that immense investment has to be made in outwitting that ever watchful 'delinquent ego'.

This then was the first therapeutic requirement at Peper Harow – that a process should be established which would constantly undermine resistance to insight and change. The second requirement was to establish a lifestyle that enabled all experiences, whether of everyday life or those more specifically psychotherapeutic or educational, to come together in order to nourish emotional growth and thus compensate for the impoverishment of the youngsters' past.

Clare Winnicott approaches this emotional impoverishment and its healing from a slightly different perspective. She writes that

> All children who come our way have been through painful experiences of one kind or another and this had led many of them to clamp down on feelings and others of them to feel angry and hostile, because this is more tolerable than to feel loss and isolation. Our work, therefore, is not easy because it will lead us to seek contact with the suffering part of each child, because locked up in the suffering is each one's potential for living and for feeling love as well as feeling hate and anger.
>
> (Winnicott 1968: 69)

Mrs Winnicott emphasises, therefore, that the youngster's resistance is not merely a demonstration of his or her wilfulness, but rather a defence against the renewal of contact with the hurt within. Paradoxically, though, staff must overcome the youngster's defensiveness and actually make contact with this hurt if the youngster is ever to lay it to rest and be able to get on with an alternative life to his or her malfunctioning one. As Mrs Winnicott continues,

> To feel a sense of loss implies that something of value, something loved, is lost, otherwise there would be no loss. Awareness of loss therefore, restores the values of that which is lost and can lead in time to a reinstatement of the lost person and loving feelings in the inner life of the child. When this happens, real memories, as opposed to fantasies, of good past experiences can come flooding back and can be used to counteract the disappointments and frustrations which are also part of the lost past. In this way the past can become meaningful again. So many of the children we meet have no sense of the past and therefore they have no sense of the present and of the future.
>
> (*ibid.*)

And yet, there were also children at Peper Harow who had always been deprived of the 'valuable experiences' that form the foundations of positive psychological development. In other words, for them it was as if there were no lost good feelings to be found. Without the existence of 'good past experiences', they were left with only pre-verbalised feelings of emptiness, or confusion, or terror. These youngsters, we at Peper Harow believed, needed good present 'experiences . . . to counteract the disappointments and frustrations'. And yet whatever good experiences were available at Peper Harow, such children found it almost impossible to be nourished by them. Theirs was the classic, emotionally malnourished presentation so sombrely described in Bowlby's *Maternal Care and Mental Health* (Bowlby 1966). Their emotional life seemed to have been paralysed in infancy. What could be done in adolescence to give the growth processes of infancy a second chance?

What had been translated into the lifestyle at Finchden Manor (Burn 1956) were those very experiences that a fortunate infant receives and that are the foundation of his or her positive attitude to him- or herself and to his or her environment. That attitude is a self-valuing one, anticipating reward and success and increasingly able to risk exploration that leads to confirmation of those expectations. The form of those experiences was obviously different from what had been appropriate for a baby. What was essential was that they contributed to a sense within the individual that he or she was esteemed, loved, deserved good things and that his or her own products, however immature and crude, were still acceptable as valued contributions to his or her growing up. The particular lifestyle at Finchden appealed hugely to adolescents and to boys in particular. Despite its intriguing antique and ramshackle appearance, the standards of music, literary criticism and visual arts, for example, which it elicited from the adolescent residents were truly remarkable.

Lyward's programme used the rebellious resistance of the youngsters towards positive ends. On the one hand, the youngsters were allowed to sleep on the floor if they chose to do so, to drink out of jam jars when they had broken all the cups though, on the other hand, if they chose to wallow in unacceptable behaviour for too long then they would be challenged in the fiercest terms by that apparently permissive leader, Mr Lyward, himself. Despite his acknowledgment and acceptance of the underlying feelings which the youngsters' behaviour expressed, his object as a psychotherapist working with adolescents was to emphasise the contradiction between their behaviour and what was appropriate for their maturation. He did not reject the most unsavoury of youngsters, even when he was decrying an individual's specific behaviour. Finchden Manor seemed to be the antithesis of disciplined institutions like Borstals, or Approved Schools, whose intolerance of bad behaviour was blind to the underlying hurt that compulsive behaviour demonstrates.

Given the freedom to find the worth beneath the dross, many adolescents at Finchden became extraordinarily creative. Their transformation was remarkable, but it was not based upon magic. Examined in depth, a logical psychotherapeutic process became discernible that seemed appropriately applicable at Peper Harow too.

Given similar freedom, outside appearances at Peper Harow in its early days very rapidly duplicated the robbers' den scenario at Finchden. Given the money to buy their own clothes instead of being issued with wholesale, institutional garments, it was immediately misappropriated to be spent, perhaps, on drink. Soon youngsters were seen in ragged jeans and barefoot, with long hair, choosing to spend on cigarettes money that should otherwise have been saved for haircuts, shampoo and clothes. They too shocked visitors, drinking out of jam jars. Allowed to express themselves as they wished, the unfurnished bedrooms and huge public rooms of state began to resemble art colleges of the 1960s rather than a Grade 1 listed building!

Electronic music equipment was purchased, abused, repurchased and destroyed, until there was no money left to replace it. But by that time, pleasure in music-making and in other creative activity had become valued by the youngsters who had thus developed a vested interest in becoming less destructive. Perhaps acoustic guitars rather than electric ones could be purchased and money even found for lessons! Music for its own sake, rather than for the acting out of fantasy through the wielding of million-watt amplified noise, had taken root. Given a freezing winter, their own cold feet asked less easily deniable questions about whether their clothing money had been appropriately spent! At the same time, they were also clear that they were valued, loved even, by the staff, irrespective of their behaviour. By then, they were also becoming curious to understand why they were so destructive, especially towards themselves. Therapeutic objectives of growth and change were no longer only the staff's objectives: they had become goals shared with the youngsters too. Only when this occurs can psychotherapy become effective. However essential the need for change seems to others, the motivation must come from the individual.

Transition takes time. For the predominant functioning of a group to move from a neurotic and delinquent base to one based on positive adult values, a lengthy period of ambivalence with much appalling behaviour, interspersed with despair, inevitably occurs. It takes time for the group to test whether it is really loved for itself, or whether it gains approval only when its behaviour pleases the adults. Are the youngsters expected to be merely compliant, or is the emotionality of the whole Community to be shared between adults and youngsters, as in a growth-promoting family? If the transition is successful, a peer-group culture is established that will enable an individual's resistance to be overcome. In the expectation that this would eventually occur, a daily Large Group was established from the venture's beginning. Again it took a long time before the Large Group's potential purpose and way of functioning became sufficiently understood. To start with, it created huge anxiety as unrelieved tension increased throughout most meetings. To help to manage that tension, Small Groups were set up as well. It was hoped that eventually these would become traditional psychotherapy groups. Both kinds of group were also envisaged as teaching situations for new staff.

Most staff were young, educated to at least degree level, modest and realistic about their ability to develop the skills they lacked and above all, they were immensely hard-working and endlessly enthusiastic. Every member of staff took personal responsibility for the overall situation of three or four youngsters. During their four or five years together, both member of staff and youngster recognised that they were each growing in ways that were mutually important. The member of staff was at first like an older brother or sister, hugely supportive, great fun to be with and meticulously enthusiastic about their youngsters' wellbeing. With time, as their knowledge deepened, their sensitivity sharpened, and under constant supervision their therapeutic skill became effective.

Psychotherapy was presented in a variety of ways. It is never easy to put something right that has gone wrong, so it was not surprising that our best intentions were not inevitably successful. Both individual and group work were not always good enough by themselves to meet the need. However, the psychotherapeutic objectives did not depend only on one or two kinds of resource. They were seen as extending to every aspect of community life. Every youngster was part of a kaleidoscope of changing informal groups, each of which simultaneously demonstrated both the difficulties and the emerging creativity of the youngsters. Great interpersonal sensitivity was shown by the youngsters in their shared bedroom situations, though when staff were less visible much delinquent activity inevitably expressed itself too. Once formal education began to develop, a youngster's Study Group, aware of his or her difficulties, could lend its active support to make sure that the fragile student did not become overwhelmed by anxiety. The peer group itself could prevent such an individual either withdrawing, or disrupting the lesson. This peer-group management of an individual's behavioural difficulties was especially evident in camping and expedition activities. Because an individual's inappropriate responses to difficulty were contained, he or she therefore remained accessible to the opportunities which each situation offered instead of wasting them.

Within such an environment, interpersonal relationships are obviously the most important factor. The peer group and the staff at Peper Harow actually did have the mutual strength to support and contain behaviour. Nevertheless, the problem of the individual's profound resistance to remembering the past, or to tolerating depression and grief, or to managing anxiety engendered by caring about someone who might reject them – such experiences remained exceptionally difficult.

After the first three or four years, we also began to suspect that there was more potential in the repeated daily physical experiences than had initially seemed apparent. Considering what unsettled feelings so many youngsters had and what institutionalised or deprived mothering they had also experienced, we speculated as to whether the feeding situations of the here and now and the bathrooms and lavatories could be specifically designed in order to induce feelings that had not been experienced before. We began to recognise that the very materials from which the furniture was made could themselves make a symbolic statement. Tables that appeared to be made from solid wood did not on examination turn out, deceptively, to be made from veneered blockboard, or even plastic! Things were really as they seemed and could be trusted. For all that, many youngsters still seemed only able to see their surroundings, even the intrinsically beautiful park, for instance, as menacing and bad. However, if the daily material experiences could be designed to produce a pleasurable reaction, we hoped this would tend to counter sour paranoia and help the individual to recognise the good reality in the world around them and also begin to recognise that they really were entitled to this too. Cooking and cleaning were situations which emphasised the relationship between the environment and the individual. Not surprisingly, these developments were not universally welcomed, but then the 'delinquent ego' was always on the look-out for any identifiable intention to change the way individuals felt about themselves.

Perhaps the most successful indicator of change for the individual was illustrated by the development of education and by its increasingly successful examination outcome during the period that concerns this study. It should be emphasised that exams were not regarded as evidence of success in themselves. However, their existence is at least concrete. The results are astounding! Of the sample, 77 per cent passed a variety of public examinations at 'O' and 'A' level. Of the research sample, 38 per cent actually went on to university while a further 12 per cent also graduated to other tertiary or vocational courses. Almost everyone learned a musical instrument and the end of term concerts became increasingly impressive and moving occasions. Hard-won skills stimulated further motivation, generated the interpersonal exchange of positive feelings and hope, and by doing so helped to restore their functioning in depth. A most important fact is that youngsters who had been unable to learn when they came and who found immense difficulty in recognising cause and consequence, had become capable of consistent study. To conceive of a sculpture, for instance and be able, over many months, to learn how to form it from a material, having acquired the specialised skill to do so, might arguably be possible for most adolescents. Our youngsters, however, had not developed the optimistic anticipation of success, the ability to face a difficult task without being thrown into anxiety and panic. Instead, they had developed a series of perverse strategies that would actually prevent their development. Many could barely read and write when they first came. For such youngsters to go to university when they left Peper Harow has to be an indicator that something had transformed their functioning.

Lyward always said that disturbed youngsters should not be pressurised into education, because when they were ready they could learn much more quickly than normal. And so we found. We recognised from the start that the youngster first needed to suspect at least that he or she was entitled to do well, to be the kind of person capable of being knowledgeable,

22

capable of communication, capable of differentiating truth from falsity, worthy of the respect of teachers. In other words, some therapeutic development needed to have taken place before success in formal education could have become possible. The foundation for this development normally lies in the stimulating and encouraging environment of babyhood, which is why newcomers were encouraged to relax and play. There was little pressure upon them to do more than get up and attend the daily Community Meeting, attend their weekly Small Group and their basic hour with their member of staff and probably spend three or four hours of one day per week helping with the cleaning or with the cooking.

Exploring the grounds was encouraged by other youngsters only a little more senior. Their activity was like that of seven- and eight-year-olds. Their playing in the mud by the marsh and in the river might well settle down into a still younger mode of play. The Foundation Studio provided the opportunity to play with tactile materials under the maternal encouragement of staff, though always without any compulsion to attend. Meanwhile, the heedless youngster could not help being aware of the concentrated activity in the studios next door to the Foundation Studio, or in the prestigious Library − or of lessons in the Dining Room between meals, or wherever more senior residents felt comfortable.

But as well as the unspoken encouragement to reinstate earlier developmental learning processes through play and apart from the tacit pressure of senior peer-group example, perhaps the most considerable psychotherapeutic/educational development at Peper Harow was of language. Clare Winnicott describes loss of language as a major feature of disturbed children (Winnicott 1968: 66–67). The use of language initially derives from a positive relationship with the mother. Its development, some would suggest, may also be organically promoted (Sacks 1989) but this may be impeded by emotional disturbance.

At Peper Harow, from its earliest days, we could not fail to recognise everyone's sudden expansion of language skills during their first two years. Youngsters were desperate to be accepted by their peer group, but they needed the common understanding of what was being said and of what was going on around them. From the morning Community Meeting to the discussion in the dark after lights out, conversation occurred. It would have been interesting to have compared the rate of language acquisition after a year of this intensity of discussion, about issues that mattered most to adolescents, with the rate of improvement in a school in which English was studied for seven 40-minute periods per week. At Peper Harow, youngsters who could barely read and write and whose conceptual linguistic ability was extremely limited, managed to obtain university entrance qualifications after two or three years of formal study. In secondary education, seven years is deemed necessary for this and then only after eleven years of pre-school and primary preparation. Our youngsters received about two years' preparatory educational nurture and then perhaps another two or three years of study, which they had usually by then come to believe was a privilege to be earned by genuine commitment. We were sure that emotional preparation for age-appropriate learning is an essential precursor to motivation. Without emotional readiness, learning is almost impossible.

Similarly, without personal recognition of need and without personal choice, psychotherapy is not possible either. Therefore, a youngster's initial contact with such an unexpected lifestyle was intended to shock him or her out of their habitual defences. The whole object of the vast effort invested in setting up an interview, its preparation and follow-up was to get the youngster himself or herself to make the choice to come to Peper Harow. From our discussions with the referring agency, we had already agreed that the youngster needed Peper Harow's psychosocial treatment process – and this decision was not in any way based upon a supposed IQ score. However, perhaps because visitors were impressed by the verbal and creative skills of the Community, it was regularly assumed that we looked for youngsters with high IQs. Internal investigation during the 1970s of pre-referral Wechsler Intelligence Scale for Children scores, demonstrated only the normal population IQ span, except for those below 85 (average 100). Independent researchers, at another specific time in the mid-1970s, had found an IQ average of 'borderline superior' (Millham, Bullock and Hosie 1978: 165). However, our fundamental concern, around which we designed the youngster's initial interview, was to look for his or her potential to engage with the Community's therapeutic objectives. We hoped that the interview process would arouse his or her curiosity in that objective, making this experience the first step on the road.

HAMISH I didn't really understand what Peper Harow was when I went there. Part of me was blocking it out. I was desperate to please my mother and my stepfather. I went to desperate lengths to achieve this.

My stepfather was actually at the interview . . . When I was actually offered a place I refused it. I talked about it with my stepfather on the train back and I decided that I would go. He was in favour of me going. I don't suppose that there was anything altruistic in his motives. He just wanted to get rid of me, I suppose.

It was essential that Hamish chose to go. That he was ambivalent about leaving home and uncertain as to what might reassure him was far less important. At Peper Harow, we realised from the first that the youngster's resistance to his or her initial awareness of reality and commitment to change would soon return and then that their unacceptable behaviour would have to be managed. A way would have to be found to overcome that resistance, without confusing their psychotherapeutic need with their social need for discipline. If the very first contact Peper Harow made with each youngster could engage their interest in their own welfare and could reassure them that what was available in the Community would not – indeed, could not – be imposed on them, then this initial interview experience could be used for reinforcement whenever conflict about their commitment arose during their stay.

Engaging the youngster in an adult process was an important reason for inviting him or her to an interview. If the social worker felt that the presence of his or her family would not actually be counter-productive, we encouraged them to come too so that they would get some idea of our values and of what we did, and also in order to counter the possibility of their undermining our relationship with their youngster.

We already knew from the case papers that the youngster needed help badly, but we wanted them to have some experience of what that help might be like at Peper Harow. And, after all that unfamiliar experience, we still wanted them to make the positive choice to come themselves. Their whole day was designed to this end. They were met initially by two youngsters who, it was hoped, would reassure the newcomer that despite all their problems and their frequently shameful behaviour, they could come to believe in their own worth at Peper Harow.

The interviewee, his or her family, putative staff member and the two residents ate together with the Community and so observed how the youngsters and the staff interacted. In the afternoon, they themselves became the focus of a lengthy psychodynamic group process, whose object was to make them feel valued but also to confront them with the painful reality of their situation. Then, having been offered a place, they were asked to go away and write if they wanted to come. Most were too anxious to be able to reflect about anything and they had already made a decision based upon impulse. Nevertheless, their first actual contact was already teaching them a lesson about an unfamiliar lifestyle and about a more optimistic way of dealing with their problems.

RUPERT The interview was really, really intense. My mum was in tears and my dad wasn't saying anything. I said, 'You can see what's going on. You can feel it.' It was gut-wrenchingly tense. I can't remember if I was in tears. I felt like it. In those days, I couldn't cry. In that interview, I felt that there were people who might be able to help me. I thought, 'This is something! I have never seen anything like this before!'

Writing a letter might be their first personal reappraisal of their own psychosocial position. It was hoped that doing so would arouse their motivation to understand what was happening to them in their current life.

Many were impressed, either positively or negatively, by their first view of the house and grounds, though their own observations almost always astounded them most.

> MAX I was struck by the way the adults spoke to the residents. I was absolutely amazed by it! I'd been in the institutional care system long enough to have been treated pretty barbarically . . . so to go to Peper Harow and find adults talking to children as though they respected them was quite mind-blowing!

Not that 'talking to children as though they respected them' was necessarily comfortable. As Solly says, 'I always tried to be too clever.' At fifteen and in the presence of residents and staff who were experts in deviousness and defensiveness, Solly's attempts to impress were bound to fail. If the interview was to be a real experience of what Peper Harow might mean to Solly, it was important to show him that straight talking and respect could go together. The experience helped Solly to clarify what life he really wanted.

> SOLLY Just the few hours of the interview made a big difference. I suppose I was really looking for help . . . I suppose I saw something there that said there was a chance for me. It made me feel a bit hopeful and plus they gave you a lot of opt out clauses, like 'Stay three months and if you feel it doesn't work, you can leave.'

Seventy-nine per cent of the transcripts clearly express how significant the youngsters feel the admission procedure was. Even the 21 per cent who do not agree generally describe memories of the resistance that the experience had aroused. They were certainly not indifferent.

Eighty-two per cent say that they found the decision to agree to come to Peper Harow was fairly easy to make. For some, their decision may indeed have been prompted by despair or, as Gavin suggests, the hope that humane treatment, rather than his punitive Remand Centre, would at least make for an immediately easier life. Ben describes the experience.

> BEN I was in Hammer House Youth Remand Centre. To me it was like a concentration camp there. There were 18 foot fences with razor

wire. You were in a cell twenty-two hours a day. It was a horrific experience.

Whether or not youngsters were at this point prepared consciously and openly to acknowledge their need and to seek to engage themselves in a psychotherapeutic process, they at least made sure that they arrived. The possibility of a totally new way of addressing their unhappiness had been made available to them and they had unusually begun by accepting rather than by destroying it. Perhaps too, this had been the first time that they had been shocked into giving real attention and consideration to their psycho-social position – which was, of course, the primary object of the encounter. Wilf, during his interview, was taken aback by the director's leading him outside for a walk . . . but through his study window, rather than the door! As unconventional an adult as this might really represent a more attractive proposition, however crazy, than an institution such as the one from which Ben had just come. It was when they actually arrived that the enormity of their decision frequently hit them.

> VERA Accepting a place at Peper Harow was easy. Living there was hard.

Although Vera's choice was influenced by despair at the alternatives, others still found the demand for them to write a letter expressing their own wish to come was not easy. Some were so suspicious of adults that they could hardly believe their experience and felt the need to preserve a way out. The offer to which Solly refers that allowed them to opt out after a term was not enough. Our prime objective was to get them into Peper Harow, so that although one transcript gleefully announces that the youngster never wrote his letter, we were more concerned with getting him not to destroy a last chance than with regimental adherence to a for-mula. We offered an interview in response to initial referrals, because we were sure that the youngsters really needed what we could offer. The question was whether they would be able to make use of the opportunity.

Obviously, Peper Harow could not cope with more than the number for which it was designed. This averaged forty-five to fifty residents, which we felt was the maximum for youngsters of this age. Together with a profes-sional staff group of about nineteen, this seemed to be the largest number of people capable of knowing each other sufficiently well to achieve their common group experience. From the referral papers and, indeed, even after the interview, it was not possible to know who would eventually make a success of their opportunity and who would opt out. At best, everyone referred was ambivalent about dealing with their problems, but even those who began by denying that they had any sometimes showed, through a smile, or a brief eye contact perhaps, that they would like help if a way could be found to help them accept it. Only girls (before Peper Harow became co-educational) or those of the wrong age, or those who were diagnostically psychotic, or who would only stay under escort, were refused an interview. What we sought, above all, was the eventual possibility of motivation and that they might eventually be able to become part of the peer group. No one was selected for interview simply because of their behaviour and especially not for their amenable behaviour! No one was selected because of their IQ score. We were influenced solely by whether there was an outside chance that they could be helped by a group process, with which they might be able to engage. Thus, most referrals were offered an interview and hardly any were refused a place after this. Unfortunately substantiating figures are not available, but memory suggests that between 1970 and 1983 fewer than ten people refused a place after interview and that fewer than that were not offered a place after interview.

In the 1970s, central government was exerting considerable pressure on regional groupings of social service departments to build secure units for youngsters with apparently intractable behaviour problems. Many social service departments resisted and Peper Harow was asked to assess the case papers of the twenty-eight adolescent boys and girls in the local region who had been recommended in the previous two years for closed provision. As we were not co-educational at that time, we could not have offered a place to about a third of the group. Apart from that issue, we would have offered interviews to all but two.

As we will see, the effectiveness for nearly every resident depends on the group's strong sense of identity. Creating and nourishing this requires leadership, staff commitment and many other qualities, but it also requires a well-judged balance of what can be tolerated at any one time. Thus, ten compulsive fire-raisers in a group of forty, for example, is likely to produce too much pathology of a particular kind to be manageable. For those reasons, there might temporarily be times when interviews would not be offered to any more acting-out sex offenders, or drug addicts, or exceptionally violent youngsters (see Table 2, p. 59).

Thus, a summary of the principle of selection was that any kind of adolescent with almost any kind of difficulty might have been treatable at Peper Harow. Their ultimate success depended enormously on what the psychodynamic levels of tolerance and pathology were in the Community at the time of arrival and whether, very rarely, an individual was hell-bent on destructiveness, or on self-destruction, at that time in their life, or if they were psychotic. What this implies, of course, is that many Peper

Harows might be needed in order to be able to cope at any one time with the number of people who would benefit from the same group process. Each individual could not simply be grouped without regard to interpersonal influence. There were times when we learned this lesson the hard way. However, it could certainly not be claimed that the successful outcome which this study represents derives from any initial selection of less difficult youngsters.

> Peper Harow . . . offers a coherent treatment approach to high-risk young people. By a variety of structural features, they win high commitment from their clients and hold on to those whom others would define as in need of secure provision.
>
> (Millham, Bullock and Hosie 1978: 171)

3

BEFORE AND AFTER

As we have seen, the real problem that youngsters brought to Peper Harow was not their anti-social behaviour. The greater problem was that they were actually unable to respond appropriately to the normal constraints of every-day life because of their inadequate or damaged psychological development.

The first four of the following descriptions by ex-residents illustrate a variety of problems and behaviour. The transcripts frequently demon-strate the insight that has derived from the ex-resident's years of hard-won experience and from the maturation of their own personality. What still seems especially difficult for the participants in this study to acknowledge fully is the hurt and loss which their more extreme circumstances had caused them. It seems equally difficult for them to recognise how bizarre their behaviour actually was before and when they first arrived at Peper Harow. This phenomenon will be discussed more fully later. However, for the present, it may prove instructive simply to read what they themselves say about their past and about their behaviour before and just after they came to Peper Harow.

> HENRY I was the eldest of four children. I and my sister were originally in care when I was aged two. It was a pattern of sporadic contact with my family until we were taken into care again. Finally, I went into care at five until eleven. I went back home and started to get into all sorts of trouble. I was put in Remand Centres. Between the ages of eleven and thirteen I was called 'out of control'. There were several stops in Remand Centres . . . where I learned a lot more about criminal behav-iour than I was supposed to.
>
> When I was fourteen, I was seen by a consultant psychologist and they decided that I wasn't insane, which was what they wanted to label me as. In fact, I was relatively unhappy and reasonably intelligent.

I never had much contact with my mother as a child. I viewed her with a certain amount of negativity and my stepfather I certainly haven't seen. He's the guy that used to beat up the children. Not so much me after I had a massive fight with him when I was about twelve. I actually beat him up, which was a strange experience for a young child. I tried my hardest to stay out of his way.

There was a very big guy who felt that he could bully me and he did attack me. I ended in a massive fight with him. What was worrying was how much I found myself enjoying it. That gave me food for thought. I actually hurt him quite badly and he didn't try it again. I lost two teeth, so there was a price to pay.

Some people felt that I was older than my years at the time and I was living a very maverick lifestyle. I never really got into a lot of criminal trouble in the early days. I wasn't really interested in that apart from the odd going along with the lads and breaking in somewhere. I never was interested in that myself. The major things were not being at school and if someone tried to get me to do something that I didn't want, I just lashed out or became quite violent.

In my early days [at Peper Harow], people didn't want to tangle with me. That was one of the reasons that I was there. I used to design weird and wonderful weapons, razors stuck on the end of broomsticks, for example. Walking around with these used to terrify the staff and sent people scurrying for cover.

WILFRED I have a family I don't see. It's been like that since I left home in 1970. They are not real family, because I was adopted to start with. It was a difficult adoption, because of the way that my adoptive mother felt about me. I reminded her of all the kids she'd had that had died. She'd had three unsuccessful pregnancies and was told that she could not have children. She then adopted me, because her sister knew my mother. We never really got on particularly well. I had a very difficult time when I was young. She physically and verbally abused me. She beat me up a lot of the time. I don't feel that there is any love lost.

Prior to going to Peper Harow, I didn't feel that I had much going for me. I felt mentally and physically and intellectually inferior to most people. I hadn't really developed very much. I had been forced to sit in cold storage, because of the things that had happened to me. They made me feel fairly insular and cold and cut off.

There was that much anger. It was pretty devastating stuff. She used to beat me with all sorts of implements, take knives to me and so

31

on. I've never felt particularly good about those childhood experiences. I woke up to find her trying to smother me under my pillow.

I was forced to fight back once, about four months before I left home. She was trying to attack me with a poker and I kicked her hard enough to break her arm. I thought it was the only way out. She developed internal bleeding and the whole of her side swelled up. It was all blue and fairly disgusting. That was the only time I resorted to that sort of violence in self-defence. She had been in and out of mental hospitals and obviously needed some sort of help. She used to beat my dad up as well. I used to wake up and hear her beating him as well. I could hear him crying.

Unusually, I wasn't in care. There were a few situations that I had got into with some delinquent school-friends of mine. We used to do petty burglaries and the usual stuff like robbing the local ice-cream factory. There was nothing serious. When I did go to court, I was very lucky. With the reports from my school and my teachers and his own insight, the judge worked out that I didn't need a punitive institution, I needed a supportive agency to get involved.

JOSH Before Peper Harow, I was a bit violent and aggressive from an early age. It's all a bit murky still. Problems started from about ten onwards and that was when the problems started arising with my parents. But from then on, if I pissed my mum off, she would say to my dad, 'Give him a beating for us', and he would. That's a bit exaggerated, but something like it. Now I think that he didn't entirely want to, but he was like that, and that did rub off on me. My tantrums were not stamping my feet, but throwing a hoover across the room. That was what it was like.

I didn't have many friends. It wasn't a normal upbringing at all. My mum tried to get me into the Cubs and the Scouts, but there wasn't any support or love at home. I have talked about this with my sister in the past. They fed us and clothed us and sent us to school . . .

I was accused of being a bully at school, but my idea of a bully is a nasty person. I was a bit boisterous. I have thought about this before. I was a bit of a bully. I have to admit it. But I wasn't extreme. I was just a bit rough with people smaller than me. I don't class myself as a bully. I suppose I must've done, but don't remember disturbing the kids or doing anything like that.

I enjoyed myself reasonably well at primary school, although I got claustrophobic sometimes. I can remember that very vividly. I wanted to run down the corridor to get out of the building. I wanted to break out. I can always remember that.

Then as I got older I got naughtier. I started stealing cars and there was a burglary here and there. That was when the social workers started sniffing around. I worked on a farm for a while down in Barshire with a load of monks. That was fun. This is one thing that I kept secret. I had to leave because I took my anger out on the animals. I threw bricks at pigs and things like that. It got a bit nasty. I didn't kill any of them, but they were suffering. The pigs had black eyes and that sort of thing. I'm ashamed of it now . . . So I was taken away from there.

It wasn't a very normal upbringing. I always wondered why my dad didn't take me to the football, things like that. I suppose it was quite deprived.

SHARON My mum died when I was seven. I know that she was murdered. It's a very hard thing to live with, because there is nothing I can do to prove it. I have looked into it. My dad did it. There were four autopsies and she wasn't buried for nearly three weeks. But because my dad's story and his mum's story tallied completely he got away with it. The CID knew that he did it. It was in the Crown Court. I've got all the newspaper clippings. She confessed it to one of her other sons before she died. I thought, 'Give it a bit more time and he might eventually say.'

I think it was manslaughter, rather than murder. They probably had an argument and things got out of hand and he got too violent. My mother was a very possessive woman.

Me and my brother and sister were living with him at the time. My stepmother was there the night of my mum's funeral. He had been having an affair with her for a long time before mum died. My mother actually went to her workplace, what with her being dead possessive. My mum looked at her and laughed, because she was about thirty years older. She thought, 'What am I worrying for?' She couldn't believe that my dad would have an affair with her because she was so old.

Anyway, my dad married her for financial reasons. We didn't have any money. After my mother's funeral, we moved to Torchester, where they bought a house. She's got nine children that she left behind, so how the hell am I supposed to believe that she ever gave a shit about us? If she really did care, she wouldn't have been there the night of the funeral. All she wanted was my dad and that was it. She's got him now.

33

We all split up from home. I had a lot of problems at my junior school as well after my mum died. I got bullied an awful lot. I don't know why. I didn't have any good clothes any more. I used to wear things from jumble sales. I used to feel dirty and I never felt good. They were calling me 'Kizzy' and all those sort of things, as if I was a gypsy. I had a low opinion of myself anyway. My stepmother had burnt all the clothes that my mother had given us so I had nothing. That's why it hurt so much, because I already thought it about myself. They used to throw stones at me.

That was when I first went to boarding school. That lasted two weeks. Then we moved to Bradington. My sister went to one of my cousin's and I moved to another. My brother had already come up. We were in three different places. My sister moved into Aunt Iris's, where she was the only one apart from a grown-up son. I had to go and live with my cousins and there were about eight of them. It was very hard. I was very bright. I saw them with their mum and dad around them and I knew that I would never have what I really wanted, which was that bond. I knew it at that age when I was nine. I knew that feelings that they had between them would always be more special than mine. Eventually, that broke down.

Because I was a rogue, I got blamed for a lot of things that I never did, as well as some of the things that I did do. It came to light a couple of years ago, when I saw one of my cousins. My Aunt Iris told me that some of my cousins had owned up to things for which I had taken the blame. I was angry about this, because they hadn't thought about the effect it had on my life. They didn't say sorry that it had affected my faith in people.

I did one year at the senior school and then I went home for a while. This time is very confusing. I was sometimes only in a place for a few weeks, so it is difficult to remember the order of things. Then I started to believe that after I had been somewhere, it would close down because *it* couldn't cope. I went to a convent and two weeks after I was there, I got kicked out and it got shut down. Then I went to a place in Altarlake called Badger Vale. A week after I was there, they decided to shut it down. I thought it was because I was so naughty.

By then it was in me to be really bad. My dad had been interfering with me since I was nine. Sexual abuse in my life started about the age of five. It started with my headmaster at infants' school. When I had to go up to the front of the class and stand at the side of the desk, he would make me masturbate him. It didn't just happen to me.

I think now, 'How many other girls did he do that to and screw up part of their lives?'

I was sexually abused by my headmaster, my father, the taxi-driver, my uncle in Bradington. That really cracked me up. He said, 'Either you lift up your nightie, or I'm sending you home to your dad.' I thought, 'Shit, there is no way out now!' I was going to get it from him, or from my dad. So I just lifted my nightie and thought, 'I'd rather let you than him.' I did it that way. It was the best option I had then. Then I really did go haywire, because I really did have no one I could turn to. I was about ten-and-a-half, or eleven.

Dad hasn't got away with anything, because everyone must have good feelings. Deep down he probably yearns for all of his family. I know that there are mistakes that I have made in my life, big regrets that I have got . . . But I have given him every chance to rectify what he has done. He told me that it was my fault, that I was to blame for it. I'm clever enough to realise that it's not my fault. He admits doing it. He knows he did it.

When he was doing this to me, there was the good part of the family saying, 'He needs bloody castrating!' But what they don't realise when they say it, is that he's dad and I love him. My stepmother definitely knew at the time, but I didn't know that then.

My mother's side of the family say things like, 'He needs locking up and the key throwing away!' At the time, I didn't know that he had done all that stuff to my mother. They knew all the reasons. I know they are thoughtful people.

I was trapped then, because it was very difficult to say to them, 'I love my dad.' I would have felt that I was a pervert for loving him. Because by then I thought, 'I should hate him', but I knew I didn't hate him, so I was left in confusion again. I felt really disgusted with myself, because I still loved him. It was real and I won't lie to myself. It was a real feeling and I couldn't share it with anyone, or they would think I am a disgusting person, too. That ties in with the problem of me wanting people to think that I am a bad person.

I believed that I needed to see my dad as well, to get rid of *my* problem and give him back *his* problem. I've still not said it to him. He doesn't open any letters I send him and he puts the phone down if I ring him up.

The issues which these extracts from the transcripts describe, have undoubtedly had a psychologically damaging effect on the youngsters. Yet it is difficult to define the precise effect each problem has had upon each undeveloped personality; which exact kind of problem will bring development to a standstill, or which issue can be resolved by what particular treatment process. Despite the fact that this case material does not greatly help to relate cause and effect in any empirical way, it certainly widens our eyes at the thought of what it must have been like to have been one of those children enduring such experiences.

Staff at Peper Harow were also powerfully engaged by the compelling expression of the youngsters' experiences, and for them – probably for the reader too – no straightforward ideas that could resolve these would spring to mind. Staff were subject to a variety of contradictory feelings and fantasies in response to the youngsters' behaviour and confidences (Charles, Coleman and Matheson 1993). The existence of such responses was not generally acknowledged at the time when Peper Harow began. Staff absolutely need personal support, professional supervision and sophisticated training to help them cope with their own feelings and to help them cope with the youngsters' feelings. The alternative tendency is to respond to the youngsters rather as a member of the public might do, with prejudiced clichés that defensively distance the adult from those fears which the youngster's behaviour or past experiences arouse. It took some time to develop the support systems at Peper Harow that staff needed and it is an especial tribute to them that they had the exceptional integrity to be able to set their own feelings and attitudes aside while they continued their search for understanding.

As a result, when the youngsters at Peper Harow recognised that they were not being judged and when they felt that they were understood, then, at last, they became able to respond appropriately to others and to the world around them instead of remaining driven by the impulses and fantasies of their unconscious. What initiated change, therefore, was as much the staff's attitude towards the youngsters and their belief in the youngsters' innate worth and potential ability as any particular psychotherapeutic process, or even the absorbing activities of everyday life at Peper Harow. However, the staff's devotion was not an alternative to the therapeutic environment (see Chapter 2). It was equally necessary to make that environment therapeutically effective so that it became an essential element for holding all the manifold ingredients together.

It can be seen that making some kind of measurable and objective sense from disturbed behaviour is an exceptionally difficult task. Even categorising the material is not easy, but the biggest dilemma is how to interpret it objectively. Ackerman and Jahoda, in a study of a particular form of emotional disorder, define this very problem when they describe their research of the raw expression of people in psychotherapy.

This brings us to . . . the most difficult methodological problem, that of the interpretation of the necessarily uneven data. It lies in the nature of case history material that the elaboration of common basic elements is fraught with difficulties. The more detailed the information available, the more the unique qualities of each case stand out. That is why the attempt to emphasise some basic elements for the purpose of comparison always implies the potential danger of a violation of facts.

(Ackerman and Jahoda 1950: 23)

It is hard not to be shaken and appalled by the weight of the ex-residents' combined comments about their lives before Peper Harow and the problems these experiences and events caused. Therefore it is as hard a task for the researcher as it was for the staff, as Ackerman and Jahoda suggest, to retain objectivity when trying to interpret the different levels of meaning of the ex-residents' comments. Broad themes do emerge. The ex-residents absolutely agree on the value of their experience at Peper Harow, for instance, but when we examine this more closely its significance varies from individual to individual. This is illustrated by the three following examples. The first example, Hamish, would undoubtedly be regarded as successful. Lenny, who follows, expresses quite a lot of anxiety as to whether he has at last managed to match up to his normal adult aspirations – and with good reason. Perhaps he would agree that, although he is managing, his position is only just balancing rather than being well-rooted. Albert is still struggling. He has very positive assets in his life such as Val, his wife, and his children but he still suffers seriously from a poor sense of self-worth. However, the more one considers what each of them say, the easier it is to recognise that the ability to struggle is certainly courageous and is a real psychological strength – albeit difficult to measure precisely.

HAMISH

Current situation

Life is treating me pretty good. I'm married to Trish. We met when I first started work. We have a nice house, near Trish's family, and two children. I'm in charge of Public Relations for Mornesbury Council, a job that I'm really enjoying. We see my father, but not my mother or half-sister, unfortunately. All in all, I'm very happy at the moment.

Life pre-Peper Harow

My parents divorced when I was eleven and my father went out of my life at that point. I'm no longer in touch with my mother, which is a decision she made, which was a shame. I had been trying for some time to bridge whatever gaps were there, but those gaps were unbridgeable. We invited her to our wedding, at which point she put the shutters down completely. I think that she couldn't cope with the idea of my father being at the wedding as well. Her way of dealing with it was to completely pull down the shutters and that was it.

The history is that my parents married in 1957 when I was born, both of them from Catholic families. I was conceived out of wedlock and they *had* to get married. That lasted until I was eleven, when they split up and my mother got remarried to a man who was older than her. They had a child, Maraid, and I was very much the cuckoo in the nest.

I wasn't helped by the fact that my stepfather abused me sexually and physically. I desperately wanted to make things right. My mother told me that my father was a psychopath. I came up with the very juvenile idea that I was a psychopath also. I had inherited it from my father. This made me extremely miserable. I was visibly out of control. There was no way I could control the situation. Every time I tried to make things good at home, it would all backfire, there would be a huge row and I would end up getting hit.

To be fair, my mother had emotional problems of her own and she had spent some time in psychiatric hospitals recovering from a nervous breakdown. At the age of fourteen I was on tranquillisers, things were so bad at home.

In November '73, just before I went to Peper Harow, things had got so bad I actually took an overdose. I'd been put on tranquillisers and sleeping pills and I overdosed one night, purely because it had all got too much. I woke up the next day and went to school. I looked pretty dreadful apparently, because a friend of mine said, 'What's happened to you?', so I told him. I remember not being at school for the rest of the day. I was taken away fairly soon after that and put in a psychiatric hospital in Thornbury and I stayed there for four months.

I was a depressed little boy. They tried loads of things. They actually increased the dosage of my medication ten times. It didn't do anything, it just made me sleepy. So they did what all right-thinking psychiatrists did in those days and gave me a course of ECT.

A lot of these things are still very fresh in my mind. But I still seem to be a very different person to then. It's difficult to believe that those things actually happened. But also I had a feeling that what happened was quite normal, because that's my experience and I don't know any other really. I've begun to learn about other experiences, basically through being married to Trish, who comes from a very stable background. She still gasps when I tell her about things that happened to me.

Developing relationships and self-image

Family

I was in contact with my family whilst I was at Peper Harow and also with my nanna. There had been rifts between my mother and her, but I had always managed to maintain contact with both of them. When my sister was three-and-a-half, she was put into care and she was fostered by a family that went to Southshire, so my mother didn't see Maraid for some considerable time. It was only when I left Peper Harow that Maraid arrived in a children's home in Thornbury and they managed to get things back together.

Before I left Peper Harow, my mother knew that I had been in contact with my dad because I told her. I didn't tell her when I was going to see him. There came a time when I had to decide who I was going to stay with after I left Peper Harow and I had to tell my mother that I was going to stay with my dad. I think that was tough on her, but she said she expected me to say that. Her own emotional position was fairly poor. She was quite fragile and still on medication. She had nothing to offer, whereas my father did. He had a car and he was happy and he was settled.

I had a very strong fear that if I went home to my mother, I would start to unravel again. It was a situation over which I had no control. I had tried to exercise some control over it and I felt I had a duty to manage the situation. I felt that when I left that there was nothing I could do to help the situation. I knew that if I left Peper Harow to live with her, I would simply have to endure it.

Things did disintegrate a bit. It was all a bit tense. I used to go and see her every Saturday and did a lot of work on her house. She lived down the road in Ravington which was not an easy place to get to. We spent some time together. We shared a lot of interests and it was quite good.

Then Maraid came back and she was very hostile towards me and it became painful to go there and I didn't go so much. Things had got strained before that and I had been going less often. I think what had

39

gone on was that Maraid and mother had chatted and mother has a great capacity to invent stories to justify her own feelings. She had decided that I was particularly evil and that was it. Very much as she had with my father.

It was very upsetting. Christmas '86, I phoned them up and said, 'Can I come over?' and they kept cutting me off. So I left it. I sent her a birthday card the following January and she returned it with a horrible letter saying, 'Stay out of our lives!' Trish was absolutely furious and wrote a letter back saying, 'How could you do this?'

My grandmother became ill with cancer and we were trying to support her as best we could. She went into hospital and eventually she had to go into a nursing home. I had to arrange all that. It was a big strain for me and I was doing a professional qualification for work at the time. I knew she was dying and I had to dispose of her worldly goods. My mother brought a solicitor on to me for removing them. My grandmother was suffering from Alzheimer's as well. I wrote to tell my mother where she was, because I felt I had a duty to do that. We had to go through the courts. It was awful. I got my solicitor to deal with her after that. When my grandmother died, there was a huge thing about the funeral and the whole thing was absolutely dreadful.

I don't have to cope with that now. Trish has been very supportive and my father as well. I am now the proud father of two.

Education at Peper Harow

Outcome

All my exams have different dates compared with, for example, my wife who did five 'O' levels and two years later did three 'A' levels. My education happened in a very different, more gradual way and although I don't feel inadequate about it, I am aware of it. I think that I did the best I could.

I started work on a 'Special Temporary Employment Programme'. I knew that I was only going to be at work for a year, because I had a place at Ryeminster University. I needed to find some work for that year just to do something before I went to university. An opportunity came up to work for Community Service Volunteers. They had a project going on in Watcaster, which was teaching Community education to children as part of CSV. I was taken on as Schools' Liaison Officer, which meant doing some teaching and organising the training sessions for the kids who were on the course. It was in a church in the centre of Watcaster. I was there for six months. The project closed down and I then got a clerical job working on computers for the government, working for the Factory Inspectorate. This was another six-month job which was perfect for me.

I had a good time after the first eighteen months of the English degree. Everyone was very keen, I was very conscientious and enjoyed what I was doing. I had ambitions to be a writer and I thought that by studying the great writers I would become a better writer. I don't think that it works that way. After about eighteen months, I started having a good time and my second year was enormous fun. In my third year, I realised that I had to do some work. I had lost a bit of pace by then. I knew after eighteen months that I wasn't suited to academic work.

When I got back from university with a degree and no job, I cast around for a while and never really came up with anything. I decided to write an article for a locally based . . . magazine. A week later the editor asked me to come down. He refused the article, but commissioned two others. From there work just slowly built up. I became a sort of freelance journalist but there was never enough there to sustain a life. It was fun. After a year, I made myself indispensable and I was offered a fulltime job and within two years I was actually editing the magazine myself. Being the editor was good fun, but it wasn't enough to pay the mortgage that I wanted, so I left and started again. I wasn't sure what I wanted to do.

I was offered a job training youngsters on the YTS programme. I was training co-ordinator. I was there for six months and then saw a public relations job . . . and applied. I seemed to have what they wanted and I got the job. I was there for seven years until I moved to Mornesbury, where I now run the Public Relations Department.

You now and your reflections of you then

Problem areas

I said that life was fine at the moment. I get depressed at times, especially about work. But I don't like doing things wrong at work. But I have a lot of things going for me. I live in a nice house. I am really happy with my wife. I have two kids who I am absolutely beside myself about. Things are great!

I still get very angry with myself when I make mistakes and maybe that's a throwback to me wanting to be perfect.

I have regrets. I missed out on so much life with my father. I missed a very crucial part of my life in adolescence, which we never went through. I've never rebelled. We've never tested each other out. We've never rowed. He just vanished because he thought it was best for me that he should just leave me alone to grow up. My kids will be testing me out one day and that will be unknown territory. I don't know how I will handle that.

I have times of low esteem. I had to move from my last job because I felt that the conditions weren't doing my self-esteem any good. I felt that people didn't appreciate what I was trying to do. I felt that I could do better. So it was important for me to change jobs. Sometimes I do have a problem with self-esteem which is something I have always had.

I do still get bouts of depression. I can't say if these are normal depressions, or if they are special to me because of my background. I think everyone gets low at times.

I left university and I couldn't get a job and I was getting desperate. My father and stepmother would go out to work and I would be alone in the house. Trish was working. There was one particular day when things were particularly bad. I was very low. I hadn't seen Trish. My dad came in for the evening and he said that they were going off for a drink and was I coming? I said, 'No, I'm going for a walk to clear my head.' I put my coat on and I walked and walked and walked. I walked for about two hours. It was raining gently. I suddenly became aware that I was on a housing estate where we had lived before my parents had got divorced, my old territory as a child. A police car pulls up and the guy says, 'Where are you going?' I told him that I had been out for a walk and I was going home now and that I didn't need a lift.

It was bit frightening. I hadn't been in a depression like that since before I went to Peper Harow. That really brought me up sharp. I realised that I had to do something, so the next day I got the typewriter out and wrote an article for the magazine and the rest is history.

It was that that really surprised me. I was peering over the edge again. I was able to say, 'Right! That's it. This is what I am going to do.' The depression hasn't happened since even though we've had our ups and downs like everyone. Trish is still very much my best friend.

Aspects pleased with

My family is really important. For a very long time, I could not see myself having a stable family life. When I first met Trish I was not exactly bitter, but certainly wary of relationships. I couldn't ever imagine making the commitment of marriage and having children, having seen my parents break up. Maybe that is why it took us eight years to get married. Having said from the age of fifteen that I was never going to get married and finding myself married and wanting to be married, is good. My lifestyle is OK.

Peper Harow is very much part of my marriage. We have had the normal amount of arguments and sometimes one of us has done something that the other doesn't like. With me, having been at Peper Harow and involved in so much discussion, I was able to say, 'We are going to have to talk about this'. . . . It's been of great benefit to us. Because when we have problems, we've been able to talk them out. That has been the secret of our success.

Children

I have started to come to terms with the idea that it is possible to grow up and not be hurt by your parents. I hope my kids are getting the benefit of this.

Getting by without Peper Harow

I wouldn't have been able to get by without Peper Harow. I perhaps would've overdosed. I had no aspirations. I had no idea of what I wanted to do with myself. I only knew that I was unhappy and that I was in a situation in which I had no control. I felt that I was criminally insane. I was A Bad Person. There was nothing I could do to change it and the rest of my life was going to be one misery after another.

Though Hamish's transcript reveals very little about his first eleven years, what there is suggests long-term mental health problems within the family culminating in the final marriage breakdown. Hamish states that he was sexually and physically abused by his stepfather. Recent researches suggest that a combination of violence and sexual abuse are most likely to produce the worst consequences for mental health later (Johnson and Aoki 1993: 8–10). But even in early adolescence he had already made three suicide attempts and had required hospitalisation with major medical intervention.

Yet there is much else to suggest that remarkable though Hamish's change has been during his adolescence, it is indeed a real one. His attainments of high academic and professional qualifications do not in themselves guarantee automatic entry to successful living, but the many-faceted personality strengths that must have been developed for such achievements deserve emphasis. Their existence is further confirmed by his actual work record, or rather, the kind of approach that underpins it.

Hamish's description of his family struggles, and in particular what he says about the nature of his relationship with his wife and children, suggest an emotional stance and a psychosexual identity quite different from what one might have expected, given the description of the nature of the relationship with his mother.

Finally, although Hamish expresses some doubts about his capacity to cope with depression, the development of his ability to manage this feature, together with his self-awareness, should surely be encouraging to him. He demonstrates a sense of self-esteem sufficiently well-rooted for him to base major activities, both in terms of his closest relationship and in terms of his work, upon it. He certainly demonstrates the ability to love and to work compatibly with well-adjusted maturity. The contrast between 'before and after' seems clear, beyond what one might have reasonably hoped for.

LENNY

Current situation

I am getting on fine now. It wasn't too good when I left Peper Harow and things got steadily worse to a point where they began slowly to get better. That is down to me. I always think that Peper Harow gave you the ingredients for doing something, but couldn't make you do it. You had to go on and then do it yourself.

When I left I was told to stay another year, but didn't because most of my friends had left. They had gone to university. I think that one thing I never really dealt with was relationships and losing people and being close to people. That was a real problem. I think that by the time that I left Peper Harow, I should have been able to deal with all that . . .

I've been in prison, I've tried to kill myself, I've been addicted to drugs. A lot hasn't been very good, but a lot has been good. A lot has been terrible. I admit it. I have to face up to knowing what I have done. Even with those experiences it hasn't made me any wiser. I know that if I hadn't gone to Peper Harow, I wouldn't have survived past fifteen. No way. I didn't want to live. I didn't want the situation that I was in, even though it was pretty much of my making. All the pointers were there at

Peper Harow and it was up to me to do it. I got a very, very long way there.

Relationships had always been a problem for me at Peper Harow. It was never a problem when it was purely a 'mate' relationship. If you were trying to help someone, that wasn't a problem. It was with really close relationships, where you had a real friend. I found it very hard to share anything. I found it very difficult to handle rejection, like anyone else does. I was always thinking that I was going to be rejected. I never really knew what that was about. I always thought that it was just me and my temperament when I was there.

That went on after I left Peper Harow and it affected my relationships with women. There was some very, very bad relationships. I lived with the sister of Frank Green, who was at Peper Harow. We had a child. It was always debatable if it was my child, but my name was on the birth certificate. She killed herself a year or so after we split up. I think that even to this day, that leaves me with a guilty conscience about that situation, even though I wasn't with her and it was nothing to do with me. I found that out quite a while afterwards. It's still something that I tend to brood on sometimes. But it really wasn't my fault and the way that she was wasn't my fault. The way the relationship split was probably my fault as much as hers, but I couldn't have control over the way she was.

I used to latch on to people. Most people get to know each other before they sleep together. But with me, it was always that I wanted to cling to someone for support and then if it worked out, fine. If it didn't, I would just have to cope with it. It left me with a lot of problems. I think that by doing all that I went backwards. I really went back almost to the state that I was in when I first went to Peper Harow. You can lose so much of yourself that you can go right back and destroy everything . . .

The extra year at Peper Harow would've made all the difference. I've had psychiatric treatment since I left Peper Harow and I always come away with a report saying, 'There's nothing psychiatrically wrong with you.' I feel, 'Bloody hell! *Someone* help me!' It's been very difficult. I still think that there is a lot I could've come to terms with and dealt with in a constructive way at Peper Harow. I started finding out about a lot of that when I left. That was a problem, but you've got to keep on dealing with it. You can't give up and I haven't given up.

The prison sentence was linked with drugs. It's linked to the time I spent with Leonie. First of all I was with her sister Jean and we were in Laureland. Then Leonie came down for a weekend and she moved in. She believed that she could become invisible. She used to walk into shops where they sold booze, pick up a bottle and leave. The shopkeepers wouldn't tackle her about this because they were so dumbfounded. It was the police who came around with all that. I was growing cannabis at the time. A doctor's bag had been stolen as well. I owned up to the lot of it because Leonie already had a little girl. I was fined and I couldn't pay the fine because the income from the clocks I was making at the time just wouldn't cover it.

It just became a very difficult situation. I wasn't able to pay the fine and eventually I was taken back to court and they said, 'Very sorry, but three months'. At that time I just couldn't handle that. You spent all that time trying to do something and come away with 'O' levels and 'A' levels and you end up with something like that.

So I did three months, came out, didn't have anything to do with Leonie, because she'd gone back to Landburg. I stayed with friends. Then I went back to Landburg and found her again. In all this time there had been a lot of trouble with her going off and sleeping with x amount of people, coming back and giving me the diseases. This was very difficult, especially since she was the sister of my best friend at Peper Harow, Frank Green . . .

I wasn't in contact with my parents. They wouldn't have anything to do with me because of what had happened. It was a pretty lonely situation. I didn't know what to do and I think that the drugs started then as a way of coping. I had no one to turn to. That was it. Eventually that situation folded. Me and Leonie did split completely. I went home. I talked to my parents and started slowly putting the pieces back together. By that time it was 1981.

After a while my parents got pissed off, so I went back to Laureland. I have a sister and some friends there. I went back and it was all right. Things started working out. Again, I worked on a farm. I did a bit of this and that. I got a band together. I started off with the music. Then I met someone and moved to Furnacedale. The relationship was totally naff. It was the same relationship I'm always in. Drugs came in now and again. It was like going back to it, like an alcoholic has a glass of something and it is like carrying on from the night before.

After that I left Furnacedale and went back to my parents again. My mum was quite ill while I was there. They live in Cumbercombe. She had to have both her hips done. I came back and looked after her. I eventually came back and stayed for a while. It was very difficult at that point. When I came back I was starting to get into drugs in quite a major way, things like 'speed'. Things weren't really under control. I could go over these things a lot in my mind and I never quite had the courage or the strength I needed. I don't know if it was the courage to face it or the strength to deal with it, probably a bit of both. It was just a bit too much on my own.

I still felt guilty that I was relying on my parents, being at home when my brothers and sisters were leaving home. I was the black sheep of the family, which is always a problem.

After that I did quite well. I just stopped everything and went out and got a job. I became a warehouse manager and got transferred and ended up a manager for a firm in Cumbercombe. After a few years about 1983, I did very well. I kept it together and I was on my own. Being on my own always seemed to be the way that I could sort myself out a bit.

Then I met someone else. It was a terrible thing. We got a house and everything was a disaster after that. It ended up really badly again with me having nothing and just going. Again I tried to take stock of what I had done, but it was very hard to think. For a long time I did take it out on myself and think that it is down to me. I did actually get the strength from Peper Harow to make a go of it and look at it. But when you get a reminder of someone saying, 'It's all down to you', everything gets a bit blurred. You just can't see clearly, it's all hazy.

That relationship finished. I went through the emotions again. Fell down again and picked myself up. Then I met Melissa. All this was in Cumbercombe. Ever since then things have been up and down. They are up at the moment. I don't rush myself. I don't try to do what I did before, which was say, 'Things are fantastic! Full speed ahead!' I'm more cautious now.

Obviously, I have to think about the kids. I think that in the last two years, I have really had to get myself together a lot quicker than after other times that it hasn't worked out. I'm getting there. I couldn't say that I am a hundred per cent and I'm a safe bet, but I am getting there. It's very hard to see into the future. It is still a bit one day at a time. I think that now, even more than after I left Peper Harow, I find myself being a bit unsure about myself . . .

We have two children. Alice is Melissa's child. She was about three when I came on the scene. Andrew was planned and he came shortly after. That was it then. I just went to hospital for a vasectomy. I couldn't cope with any more children. I didn't want to do what my parents did, which was to have kids until there was no floor space left.

Melissa's working and I am looking after the kids. I am a freelance musician and artist. I'm a housewife, really . . .

I got back in touch with my family again at Christmas after a long time. I think that when I left Peper Harow, they thought that I would be 'cured' and they wouldn't have to worry any more. Through getting into bad ways and stuff, I kept going back to them. The addiction to keep going back to drugs and messing up meant that I couldn't do it again. I couldn't go back and say, 'Look, I'm all right now', and then let them down again. So it took me a long time to decide that I really was all right. For their sake, as much as anything, because they are knocking on a bit. I've had to do that and they've been really good.

My dad's got cancer. It's never plain sailing. No one's ever going to say, 'Right, now that you've sorted yourself out, life can be rosy.' There's always going to be things getting in your way. He's really ill. He knows that I'm on the upward path. I've always felt with them that I'm on show. My dad was a chemical engineer and felt that art and music were for girls and 'poofs' and if you wanted to make it in the world you had to do a man's job. A man's job meant that you had made it if you were an engineer. It was a case of that. All my brothers were the same as him and I just refused, which I'm glad about.

I feel all right at the moment. It's over the last year and a half, or two years, I have found it a lot easier to deal with things. I have my bad moments, where I feel that I can't hack this after everything has gone so wrong. But at the end of the day, I do feel a lot better and I suppose that having kids helps a lot, because you do feel that you do have to give up having your own childhood eventually. I'm thirty-four and I have to think about their futures. I would hate them to go through what happened to me and to end up wanting somewhere like Peper Harow.

Life pre-Peper Harow

Life was terrible before Peper Harow. It was really miserable. It was more miserable than it's been since I left, worse than all of it put together. It was that bad. I just couldn't cope with it at all.

I am from a large family and that was part of the problem from the start. I was in the middle, the older ones were at school and the younger ones were being born. So I remember for a long time I moulded a lot of my early character on the fact that I was alone. I played on my own. A lot of the things that I have done since, like drug-taking, were always on my own. I've never done it in big groups like a lot of people do. I've never done that. It's always been on my own.

It was terrible. Part of the problem before I went there [Peper Harow] was the people that I mixed with. I just wasn't interested in people who were thirteen. I thought that they had nothing going for them. I wanted to go out with seventeen-, eighteen-, twenty-five-year-olds when I was thirteen, which is how I got into a lot of bad ways.

I think that the major things in my life then were drugs and running away and trying to upset my parents as much as I could. I was getting them back for whatever they told me, although thinking about it now, I just never saw what they did do. I was scapegoated. Once I had actually got the ball in motion and stood up a few times when I had been told to sit down, that was it. They couldn't cope with it, because my dad went away on business for a long time . . . He'd come back after a month and he'd have another son or daughter and he'd also have 'Lenny's legacy' of 'what he's done while you've been away'. They were very staunch Roman Catholics. It was always the case that you stopped having kids when you couldn't have any more. There were only seven of us, but it was enough, especially when there is only one parent running around and the other is two-and-a-half thousand miles away.

I think that my mother had had enough. She used to say, 'I want you out. I want you to go to Borstal. I want you to go, I don't care where. I hate you. I don't love you. You're a total waste of space.' I had no answer to that, so I thought, 'God! My mother thinks I'm like this', and I just got into a terrible state about it.

My mother got these guys from the Education Committee, who in those days were like having the bailiffs around. They were really heavy people and I couldn't cope with that. I used to go absolutely mental. I had a priest round to exorcise me, because I was possessed by the Devil as far as they were concerned. That did even more to make me feel that nothing was wrong with me and I had just gone off the rails a bit. I played on that one a bit when he came around. I played on *The Exorcist* routine, apart from spinning my head around 360 degrees. The curtains suffered a bit. I wasn't too happy about being locked in a room with a priest.

I actually went to a little place before Peper Harow, which was something we built up and which eventually got quite big. I was one of the first five and we decorated this hut in Cumbercombe College. It was around about that time that I did make some friends and I was a bit more responsive to things around me. It was very creative but there wasn't enough there. It was a very tight budget and a very tiny little shed. In time I just got bored of it. I wasn't really doing anything constructive, except meeting a few more runts like myself and going off and creating.

I got into Peper Harow by mere chance. My sister knew a friend . . . of Ray Dalziel [a member of staff]. My sister had said to him when she went out with him that I was having a difficult time of it and that she could see what was going to happen and that I didn't care and that my mum probably couldn't have cared if I had died at that time. I think that there is a very good chance that she would've thought, 'Thank God for that!' She would have grieved afterwards. It was that bad. I can't blame mum for that now. I can see the situation, but I didn't have any control over myself and I couldn't cope. I had the odd cry for help, but I wanted them to prove that they loved me. They were my parents and even if that meant jumping over a cliff to pull you back, they should've done it. The more I realised that they wouldn't do it, the further you go and the higher the cliffs. It just didn't work out.

By the time that I did get the interview, I had no idea. I wasn't aware of anything except whether it was light or dark when I woke up.

You now and your reflections of you then

Problem areas

I really don't think that the things that went wrong had very much to do with Peper Harow. It was a lot of my misgivings that I carried through it . . . I think that there were things that I hung onto that caused prob-lems for me. They didn't want me to leave and I shouldn't have done and I did. It will always stay with me. If I never get there totally it will be down to me. If I do, it will be down to me and to having gone to Peper Harow. It's that simple . . .

Aspects pleased with

I have two lovely children. The missus is all right. When it's good, it's great. It's hard sometimes. I don't think that I was ever destined to have an easy life, even when I was doing really well at Peper Harow. But I'll stick with it, because I do know that it's worth it. Maybe if I'd not left early, I wouldn't have had to go through all that stuff, but it was my decision and even with all that stuff I seem to have done it.

Children

Peper Harow has very much influenced the way that I am with the chil-dren. I'm not saying that I will be the perfect parent or anything. You think that after thinking that your parents were really hard on you, if you are really lenient with the kids, they will be wonderful. It doesn't work like that. It's taught me that it is a lot about talking and sharing and support. A lot of the time I felt that there was no barrier between me and the staff. I never felt, 'You're a screw!' There was a real understanding and comradeship, even though it broke down sometimes. It taught me that it doesn't matter how old your children are, you always have to be on that level with them, rather than saying, 'I'm bigger than you, so I'm going to bully you', even though you do that sometimes. On the whole, I hope that it will carry on the way things are at the moment and I hope that they will always be able to turn to me for support. I'd like them to say, 'Dad, I've done this', or, 'I'm into that.' You can be a friend. I think that one of the basic things that you learn is the comradeship and sharing.

Getting by without Peper Harow

I would be dead, either intentionally, or unintentionally. It would've been a few Valium and a bottle of whiskey. I had no chance at all. Peper Harow saved my life.

While Hamish may retain some residual doubts of his own about his emotional balance, he does seem to have acquired greater stability than many people. However, Lenny's description of his experiences since Peper Harow is far more shocking. His own regret and anguish arouses one's concern for him and it is with much relief that one comes at last to what seems his new relationship with his parents and certainly with his children and his partner, but also with himself. Lenny's success, however, is still very new. Thus the questions which his comments arouse are inevitably answered with some uncertainty.

Very early in that lengthy extract, Lenny underlines an issue of major significance both for him and in terms of how difficult rehabilitating youngsters like those at Peper Harow actually is. Lenny's special difficulty is in coping with intimacy.

Relationships had always been a problem for me at Peper Harow. It was never a problem when it was purely a 'mate' relationship. If you were trying to help someone, that wasn't a problem. It was with really close relationships, where you had a real friend.

Lenny's sense of isolation and of alienation is repeatedly emphasised throughout his story and it is hardly surprising that this distance is felt especially acutely between him and his mother. There is little factual material in Lenny's records, or in one's memory, about his infancy and yet Lenny's own descriptions of his hostility and negativity paint a very well-remembered picture that supports the probability of profound and lifelong misunderstanding between him and his mother, even if the cause is not clear.

Thus Lenny presents as someone desperately starved of affection in early life, whether this was intended or not. So it is not surprising that he would reject whatever good emotional experience he was offered from any other quarter with Pavlovian perversity. It would be typical behaviour of someone in his classic position. That Lenny could lavish sensitive insight, loyal friendship, self-sacrifice even upon others is not surprising. The corollary is that he would make sure he fails at the point of success, that he is punished for others' misdemeanours, or that, at the least, he will self-destructively be compelled to injure himself – with drugs, for example.

What then has changed? Loving others may have enabled a door to be unlocked that allows normal intimate intercourse to function. It is true that the time must eventually come when it would seem right that you should 'give up having your own childhood', as Lenny puts it. But if the remorseless emotional starvation remains unassuaged in the depths of anyone's personality, could they simply set it aside because their adult self can see what should be appropriate?

There are other examples in the extract that show how hard Lenny is trying to achieve adult maturity, contentment and self-respect. After all his years of struggle, he undoubtedly has acute insight and can at least be kind to others. These are tremendous achievements. How many people would have developed the strength to continue the struggle?

The sobering recognition which Lenny's story highlights is that although Peper Harow may have triggered a process – as Lenny generously acknowledges – its fully positive effect may require yet another decade before what the process would lead to can begin to feel certain.

ALBERT

Spontaneous comments

Current situation

I have two screaming kids and no job. It's pretty boring at the moment. We are not married, but I have been living with Val for ten years, on and off.

My children are both girls. Miriam is almost nine and Franny is almost four. I wouldn't recommend fatherhood to anyone.

I have been out of work for about four months. I was running an off-licence. I left after I had a falling out with the management. It was a clash of personalities. I haven't done anything since then. I had just bought this flat. Val works. I'm doing the childcare at the moment, but it doesn't suit me really. I'd like to get back to work. We are short of money. Val's family help us out a bit.

I haven't seen my mum for about a year. I haven't seen much of my mum since I went to Peper Harow. She didn't really want to know. I see my dad once every week or two. They divorced when I was nine. I have two sisters – a step-sister who I haven't seen, who lives with my mum, and a sister I get on quite well with. I don't see much of them. They are all quite local, within half an hour's drive, but we don't have much contact. My mum didn't want to see the kids and she never has. I don't really think it's worth the hassle to get in touch.

I'm pretty fed up with myself at the moment. Not having any money is a real drag and being at home all the time doesn't suit me. I can only hope that I get a job as soon as possible. It's so depressing just sitting indoors. You get lethargic and you don't want to do anything. I've been unemployed before, but it is different now that I have kids. I get very wound up. I managed to smash a bottle of wine when I was doing the hoovering this evening and I got upset about that.

If I had a job, it would keep my mind more active. I don't like sitting about gazing at the telly, not even watching it.

I was a bus driver, until I had a bad accident. I left because of that. I nearly got killed. I nearly got run over by a bus. I went back for a week afterwards, but I couldn't take it psychologically. The police nearly arrested me for interfering with public transport. I can still remember it now. It makes me cringe.

I think that being out of work would be a low spot for anyone. Having the kids means that I don't make as much effort as I might to find work. It's also very dispiriting to be constantly filling in application forms and sending them off and hearing nothing. It feels like a waste of time and it's difficult to get the motivation to do it . . .

Memories of Peper Harow

Peper Harow was important to me in one way that it kept me out of prison. Just before I went to Peper Harow, I spent two months inside a youth custody place (actually, its official title then was a Detention Centre) just off the A3 towards Guildford. It was meant to be a 'short, sharp shock', which was the phrase that the politicians were using at the time. I had been arrested for several crimes. Peper Harow kept me out of trouble.

Life pre–Peper Harow

I lived with my mum when my parents split up. I was running wild and I did what I wanted. She didn't give a damn. She was more concerned with my little sister or going out with blokes. She was never interested in me, so I just got in with the wrong people. No one knew what I was doing and I just got into trouble. I got expelled from every school I went to. One of the reasons that I went to Peper Harow was that Cumbercombe couldn't find a school that would take me.

I went to a special school . . . before Peper Harow. They are still around. You go up there a couple of times a week. It was for people like at Peper Harow, but in a little unit. You could talk and whatever. I would go there a couple of times a week, walk in, say hello and go home again.

Burglary and Taking and Driving Away were the crimes that I was in trouble for. I have lost count of the amount of times I have been in magistrates' courts and the number of warnings I got. They put me away in the end. A week after I came out, I was in Peper Harow. When I came out, I knew that I didn't want to go back home.

I had a probation officer, who was the only one who wanted to help me. She came down to see me whilst I was there more times than my mum and dad did. Even after I had finished seeing her, she still came down to see me.

Developing relationships and self-image

Family

My dad came down three or four times and the same with my mum in the four-and-a-half years that I was at Peper Harow. I had gone to live with my mother, so I didn't know what had happened to my dad after the divorce. He's not the kind of person to talk about it. He got brought up on a farm . . . and he is very, very old-fashioned. He doesn't like talking about his feelings. We lived with him for a little while a few years ago when we were in financial difficulty. That wasn't too good.

Sometimes I wouldn't get a birthday card or Christmas card. Mum didn't want me home. During the holidays, I'd stay in the holiday groups.

I went to France and Scotland. I'd go off to spend a week at home and I'd leave after the first couple of days. I didn't get on with my parents and I don't think that I ever will. There is the thing that your kids will be the same as you are and I will be like my mum. My dad has never been in a bit of debt, but he was never around. My mum was in a children's home and things like that and I have been exactly the same as her. It's the same cycle.

Education at Peper Harow

Education and emotional development

I've always been a bit emotional, a bit unstable and insecure. I was doing anything I wanted to from the age of ten. I was going out and stealing cars with friends. I would come home when I wanted and go to school when I wanted. I've always been on my own.

You now and your reflections of you then

Problem areas

I found things very difficult when I left. If you haven't got that much confidence and aren't that stable at times, things can be difficult. I didn't have a clue. My parents didn't want to help. When I started working . . . I would get excited about getting paid and then I would spend the money without paying the rent and things like that. I didn't know about cooking and opening bank accounts.

I've had loads of different jobs and that means that I have never been able to settle down. It's been a problem. Everything about my life has been unstable. I don't want my kids to be like me, but I find myself shouting at them for no reason. It's strange really.

Peper Harow kept me out of trouble. There were a lot of things that I liked about Peper Harow and a lot of things that I hated, like the way they set up my life. I think that's why I am still with Val. She's more of a mother figure than anything else.

We have had problems in the past. It was hard when we had problems. Val rejecting me was very much like mum rejecting a child. I really need stability, because I've never had it. I've never beaten Val up. I'm not a violent person. I haven't had a relationship with my mother, which makes it hard to have a relationship with a woman. I did go and stay with another girl for awhile. I don't know what it was. It was about not being able to have a stable relationship and never seeing a stable relationship. We've been together for ten years. We've had two break-ups. We went to counselling. It really helped. Things were impossible at the time. I felt suicidal. Life got really bad for me a couple of years ago. I got into using marijuana. I still use it now, but not as much as I did then. It isn't a problem when I'm working. When I'm not working I get so depressed. I'm not making excuses. Things are a bit bad today, the kids have been a lot of work. I was all over the place. I was so stressed.

Aspects pleased with

My kids are what I feel pleased about. I don't get on with Franny very well. I do like my kids and Val sometimes. I do feel bad about Val sometimes. She's like a mum and sometimes it's like she's looking after three kids.

Getting by without Peper Harow

I would've ended up in prison without Peper Harow. I was so much into crime. I learned a lot of criminal knowledge when I was inside.

I haven't stolen or done any burglaries since Peper Harow. I have been done for disturbing the peace and I have a lot of parking tickets. The disturbing the peace was from an argument that I had with Val. Things were really bad at that time. I hit her a couple of times, but not much. They threw me in a cell and put me in court the next morning. I pleaded not guilty. I've got a record for that.

There is so much to be read between the lines. When Albert says that he is not violent, yet talks of smacking the children and hitting Val, he exemplifies the contradictory nature of his psychosocial life. There is much in his transcript overall that demonstrates his potential intelligence and his warmth and concern for others, but his ability to form an emotionally intimate partnership with Val and to generate the persistent drive to be able to work regularly and responsibly is regularly undermined by what he calls his 'instability'. We can recognise the real difficulty of finding appropriate work in the middle of an economic depression and we can also recognise the psychological hurt caused by unemployment. Albert is sufficiently realistic to be able to differentiate between his social environment and his psychological problems.

Thus, although his current situation overall seems very fragile and is certainly no epitome of success, there are hopeful elements. The fact that he was able to obtain and be helped by counselling has especially positive implications. He shows some self-awareness and, in other parts of the transcript, perceptivity as well, particularly in his criticisms of Peper Harow. And although his working life has been wrecked more than once by his inability to cope with stress and with authority, he has managed to hold his family unit together, though we can guess how much credit for this must also be due to Val.

What both he and Lenny demonstrate, though to different degrees, is how hard it is to evaluate the worth of their experience at Peper Harow. Both would agree that it has provided some positive outcomes for them. Lenny is clear that he would have been dead without Peper Harow. Elsewhere in his interview, Albert refers to a suicidal gesture he made at Peper Harow and to his having felt suicidal more recently. His underlying despair is clear to see, but he is unable to comment on this realistically, or to connect the especially warm relationship he experienced with his special member of staff at Peper Harow with his ability to function as fully as he does as a partner and as a father. However, Albert is able to acknowledge that being kept out of prison is a pretty significant outcome.

Repeatedly, through all these transcripts, one sees the evidence of early emotional injury, from a variety of causes. There is almost no evidence of this having been recognised or treated before Peper Harow. By the time that self-destructive or grossly anti-social behaviour compels attention in adolescence, the damage to personality has been so complicating and has been overlaid by further and different injuries so many times, that real treatment has become an exceptional challenge to understanding and to any individual's therapeutic capacity. But even when these qualities are available, it may require many years – perhaps even the greater part of their lives – to achieve their maximum recovery.

Table 1 is intended to summarise how the whole sample of interviewees, including those quoted already, compares psychosocially with how they were before and during their initial few months at Peper Harow. A positive judgment of their ability to cope adequately with the inevitable stresses of adult life requires an evaluation of several broad areas of successful functioning. To have attained appropriate emotional maturity, they would have achieved a stable sense of self and they would have come to feel confident about the current direction of their life. Although they might smoke and drink, for example, they would not abuse such substances unmanageably. They might have committed minor traffic offences but they would not steal, or commit violent or other serious offences. What they say would not suggest the probability of mental health breakdown through serious depressive illnesses or suicide attempts, for instance. They would instead demonstrate age-appropriate and socially appropriate relationships with partners and children. They would also demonstrate through employed work, or educational, or artistic achievements, an ability to pursue long-term objectives and to sustain the emotional strengths necessary to attain them.

Table 1 The sample – comparative criteria

Prior to and first year at Peper Harow	Yes %	No %	*Now*	Yes %	No %
Serious emotional instability (e.g. separation; traumatisation; broken family; school phobic; clinical depression; delinquency; etc.)	100	0	*Emotional stability* (e.g. positive identity; intimate family relationships; long-term work achiever; etc.)	85	5
Expectation of success without Peper Harow (Most say: 'mental illness; suicide; addiction; crime; etc.')	24	74	*Optimistic view of own and children's future*	79	3
Effective source of emotional sustenance (No reference in any file)			*Peper Harow continues to sustain emotionally*	77	12
Positive family relationships (21 per cent of negative responses say occasionally satisfactory.)	9	85	*Positive family relationships* (Negative responses include any 'not clears')	68	32
Age-appropriate ability to work (or low attainment; truancy; expulsion; hyperactivity; etc.)	18	82	*Ability to pursue work/ educational goals* (Negative percentages include any 'not clears')	79	21

Source: transcripts and Peper Harow Files

Table 2 is collated from the reports in the ex-residents' files that were submitted as part of the referral process. It selects eleven categories of psychological and behavioural disturbance. In addition to the research participants' own comments, information is drawn mainly from the referral reports presented by Social Service Departments and schools, from Child Guidance Clinics, hospitals, Schools Psychological Services and sometimes from Assessment Centres and parents. Thus they were written by social workers, teachers, probation officers, psychologists and psychiatrists and as such they reflect a spectrum of different professional perspectives and the different professional trainings of the writers. Nevertheless, these reports provide a composite profile of the group. Each ex-resident's file usually confirms what the interviewee had himself or herself said about their past, though frequently in fuller and in different terms. Even so, some serious issues are missing altogether from their referral reports. For instance, almost 18 per cent of the sample claim to have been sexually abused as children, none of which was indicated in the referral papers. Categories have been arranged in arithmetic order of percentages. Only categories with double figures have been included. The disturbance of the pathology and behaviour of the group overall is revealed in stark terms. Table 2 emphasises still more the contrast in the residents' functioning before Peper Harow and now, as summarised in Table 1.

Table 2 A profile of ex-residents on admission

Characteristics/behaviour	%
Stealing	56
Aggressive; Hostile; Temper tantrums; violent	45
Bizarre behaviour – non-specific diagnosis	45
(e.g. suicide attempts; serious self-harm; phobic/obsessive activity; panic attacks; enuresis/encopresis; etc.)	
Bullying/Victim	38
Truancy/School phobia	35
Drug/Alcohol abuse	30
Specific psychiatric diagnosis	30
(e.g. clinical depression; psychosis; borderline personality disorder; etc.)	
Disruptive; Devious; Manipulative; Omnipotent	18
Extreme mood swings/Lacking self-control	15
Withdrawn/isolated; Incapacity for grief or independence	15
Rejection of normal social behaviour	12
(e.g. hygiene; co-operativeness; etc.)	

Source: Peper Harow Files

More than half of the group had been stealing from home or school for a long time. Nearly half of the group had also been noted as being exceptionally hostile and aggressive, with frequent outbursts of temper. A similar proportion exhibited extremely bizarre behaviour. As can be seen, nearly a third of the group suffered from a specifically diagnosable psychiatric condition.

As well as changes in their psychosocial, age-appropriate functioning, it is suggested that further evidence of the ex-residents' successful change derives from their currently optimistic view of their future and that of their children's future. In addition, there is also significant evidence of their general emotional ability to relate their past to their present lives, which demonstrates the continuation of the emotional impact on them of Peper Harow – in the same way that other people continue to be nurtured by the internalisation of good experience from earlier developmental phases in their lives.

In comparison with their optimistic view of the future and their sense of psychological sustenance from the internalised past, we can juxtapose what they now feel would have happened to them without their experience of Peper Harow. The sombre alternative would seem to have been death by some kind of misadventure, or suicide, or long-term mental ill-health, or substance addiction, or long-term criminality.

In Table 1, the interviewees' adolescent psychosocial activities (which reveal their adolescent personality development) are compared with the adult personality features described above. For instance, we might conclude that serious self-injury, or suicide attempts, or diagnosed clinical depression, or criminal behaviour, or sexual promiscuity, or bullying, or truancy or school phobia are all factors that would suggest serious emotional disturbance in childhood and in adolescence. There might be actual evidence of early physical or sexual abuse, or of the deprivation of maternal care, or of family breakdown. If some of these experiences and behaviour are recorded in the interviewees' history before and during their early days at Peper Harow, and yet those same ex-residents are now seen to have reached an appropriate adult stability, then a significant change in psychosocial functioning must have occurred. Similar comparison between the relationships within the parental family in adolescence, and with the relationships in adulthood within their own families and with their parents now that they are adult, would give some indication as to whether or not there has been a change in the essential capacity for intimate relationships. In adolescence, the ability to pursue consistent goals will be demonstrated by age-appropriate educational attainments, including evidence from functioning during activities such as expedition work at Peper Harow. Any change in capacity can be highlighted by comparing adolescent work capability with adult ability to set goals and to achieve them.

All these comparisons are summarised in percentage form in Table 1. They seem to demonstrate quite remarkable change in the group overall. However, as Ackerman and Jahoda (1950) suggest, the individual responses to questions about change at Peper Harow produced a less consistent response. This is summarised in Table 3.

Table 3 The process of positive change while at Peper Harow

How many ex-residents say there was a change in:	Yes %	No %
Relationships		
Peers and staff	71	29
Family	24	76
Behaviour	44	50
Functioning		
Engaged in arts/sports	91	6
Engaged in formal education	79	21
Link between coping with formal education and		
emotional development	62	38

It is not surprising that three-quarters of the ex-residents did not feel that their relationships with their families improved while they were at Peper Harow. Most of them feel that Peper Harow did as much as was possible as far as their families are concerned. Others feel that their families needed help as much as they did. But the breakdown between them still seems to have been unbridgeable at that time.

What perhaps is remarkable is that despite the limited improvement in this area, their current family relationships (see Table 1) are dramatically different. They must therefore, have developed some psychological strengths that underpin successful adult family relationships. It may be a reasonable speculation that Peper Harow's contribution arose particularly from their relationships with their 'gurus' and through the strengthening of their general ability to persist, to engage with peers in common objectives and in their increased awareness of personal worth. This is demonstrated in Table 3. It is hoped that Chapter 4 will help to clarify what changed and how.

61

4

AGENTS OF CHANGE

At Peper Harow it was anticipated that if the youngsters' lives were to change direction they would need to become aware of the buried feelings that promoted their attitudes and behaviour. Yet the transition from the beginning of insight to a changed way of functioning was as complex a step as the germination of insight in the first place. First of all, a real desire for change must take place even if it is not a consistent desire. Georgie typified those who, as Clare Winnicott puts it, seemed to have 'lost contact' with their past (Winnicott 1968: 69). Her motivation to recover it was certainly inconsistent.

> GEORGIE I can remember nothing of my life before Peper Harow. I went from home to home. I used to rebel against the system. I was in care when I was tiny and I went back to mum when I was seven. I couldn't handle it and put myself back in care. I was eleven. My mum beat me up and I was in hospital and I said that I didn't want to go home. They put me back in care. I was very angry.

How could this resentful and hostile child even begin to come to terms with the past, if she would let no one close to her? Most transcripts record a similarly grim personal history prior to admission.

Some ex-residents came from Assessment Centres or Remand Homes that had recommended Peper Harow to the youngster's local authority as a suitable long-term placement. They had been known to their local authorities, or to the police, for a long time. However, neither Children's Homes, nor foster homes, nor even punitive placements such as Detention Centres had managed to change the youngsters' behaviour. Social workers had been left racking their brains for somewhere that might. They rarely understood the processes that underlay the youngsters' behaviour. In addition, the youngsters' own pathology prevented their being able to recognise what caused them to feel and behave as they did. Thus, adult and youngster were both distracted by the youngster's behaviour from focusing on its cause. Roy's comment reflects this.

> ROY I got involved with officialdom for not going to school and on top of that you could say that my family was dysfunctional. There was a care order on me. I went to an Assessment Centre and I got referred to Peper Harow. At the time, the choice was to stay in hell, or go to a nice house in the country.

However, as Freud demonstrated (Freud 1938), the slips of the tongue in our everyday lives, our spontaneous humour, or the unconscious choice of even one particular word rather than another, can themselves illuminate the way an individual functions unconsciously. Such communications are often unnoticed, though it would be nonsense to draw firm conclusions from these alone. Nevertheless, Roy's inadvertent choice of words may reveal his present thoughts and feelings. For instance, using a psycho-sociologically unemotional word such as 'dysfunctional', serves to distance Roy from his feelings about his family. The need to do so may suggest that the sting of his potentially disabling, adolescent social alienation continues to be painful. His insistently spontaneous phrase, 'stay in hell', supports that suggestion, as does the instant deployment of his defensively sardonic humour to suppress such discomfort. For similar reasons it would be naive to accept at face value Roy's referral to Peper Harow as merely arising from, 'not going to school'.

The youngsters' unmanageable behaviour might include truancy, promiscuity, or self-destructive activities. Undoubtedly, bizarre behaviour certainly warranted the local authorities' concern, but what kind of treatment it seemed to cry out for and how this would work remained as mysterious as the reasons for the youngster's behaviour.

> JOSH I was in Chaingate House Assessment Centre for about seven months. I think that the animal mistreatment got back to the social workers and that's when they thought, 'We've got a bit of a case here!' That's when Peper Harow came along, which was my solution.

What Josh blandly describes as 'animal mistreatment', consisted of brutal and secret attacks on animals (Chapter 3, p. 33). Despite Josh's reputation for bullying since he first went to school, the meaning of his savage violence had been masked by his apparently paradoxical and incoherent silence. He had seemed to be a nice and simple boy!

Without having been trained to define psychological malfunctioning, social workers could not be expected to understand in what way a psychosocial treatment environment might actually resolve psychopathology.

Thus, like the general public, their response to youngsters such as Josh was based on fantasy rather than on any recognition of the match between the youngsters' psychopathology and their specific psychotherapeutic needs. At Chaingate House, understanding that sort of relationship was assumed to belong to the psychologists' specialist craft! But many mental health and educational professionals had received no psychodynamic experience as part of their training either. Psychodynamic treatment was frequently regarded as scientifically suspect, so that an environment that deliberately set out to acknowledge unconscious processes was seen as the treatment of last resort for exceptionally incomprehensible youngsters, rather than as the process of first choice for most disturbed youngsters. Only when local authorities could persuade themselves that a particular youngster was an exceptional case would they approach Peper Harow.

> HAMISH The ECT seemed to have worked . . . and someone suggested Peper Harow. I'd taken my English 'O' Level about two weeks before I took the overdose . . . but I still managed to get an 'A' grade. That knocked everyone out and they were just amazed by it. I think that was what encouraged them to send me to Peper Harow.

While this may be so, it is likely that Hamish's bizarre attempts to derail trains had also impressed the local authority that he was dangerous, or they might have accepted that ECT and pharmacology were the best solutions!

In addition, central government had strongly discouraged children's being placed a long way from home. For Hamish:

> HAMISH It was made an even tougher decision by Peper Harow being two hundred miles from home. It was quite a brave thing to do. I was sixteen, but I didn't feel sixteen.

However, in this case, Hamish's life-threatening behaviour was recognised as a higher priority. Hamish's mental state must have made his decision especially difficult. He must have feared being overwhelmed by loss – of family, of home and of any embryonic identity. He was confused as to whether his family wanted to get rid of him or whether, somehow, if he 'got rid of himself' he might, in some pathologically contorted way, be able to placate them! His interview had taken place while he was still in a psychiatric hospital after a serious overdose but, although his interview experience had persuaded him to go to Peper Harow, he could not be expected to recognise the elements of his personality conflict for a very long time. His decision to accept the offer of a place was based on impulse rather than insight, just like his behaviour.

HAMISH I came out of hospital two weeks before I was due to go to
Peper Harow – and it all happened again.

Perhaps this repeat overdose emphasised Hamish's ongoing sense of
having been rejected. He was still trying to deny that his desired family situation had long been lost. As long as he clung to that denial he was
bound to remain ambivalent about committing himself to the alternative
life he had glimpsed during his interview at Peper Harow. Because youngsters found such difficulty in acknowledging the reality of their family
situations they often agreed to accept the option of Peper Harow out of a
sense of despair at their position, rather than because they had hope or
understanding of the way it might change their life. Vera sums it all up.

VERA I don't really know how I got from a lock-up in Crowfield to Peper
Harow. I was a kid. They just *told* me, 'You *will* do this. You *will* do
that.' The place I was in was a nightmare. It was called a children's
home. It was an Assessment Centre. It was the worst place you could
think of. It was shit.
  My social worker came to see me with some papers saying, 'Have
a look at this and see what you think.' He told me what happened at
Peper Harow and asked if I wanted to go. I said, 'Yeah, all right . . .
it's a long way from home, but I'll go.'

The initial interview had been designed to circumvent the youngster's
compulsive defensiveness, so that he or she could discover that acknowledging their problems need not actually be as devastating as they had
always supposed. They were startled out of their usual reactions by the
unexpected way they were treated and by how differently from their own
previous experience the staff and other youngsters here seemed to function. They found themselves participating centrally in the discussions
about their current and future situation. Not only did Peper Harow appear
to be a good place for adolescents, who seemed to feel that they really
were understood, but their first experience demonstrated that they could
make it work for them too. The interview, therefore, had shown that psychotherapy, without overtly calling it that, was actually a joint process. Vera
was no longer required simply to do whatever she was told, nor were her
own decisions to be based on impulse.

At Peper Harow, we knew that everyday life in the residential context
can itself become the most effective agent of therapeutic change, especially
if it can be managed so as to enhance and legitimise self-esteem and pleasurable experience within the youngsters' group. Lighting fires in the
grounds or plunging among one's screaming pals into the river seemed to

be fun, in contrast with the supposedly arcane objectives of 'psychotherapy'!

VERA We had good fun on camps, because you were there to have a holiday and enjoy yourself, not really to do any work on yourself.

Although many ex-residents demonstrated unusual insight about the
way such experiences actually led to psychological change, it was primarily through becoming completely involved in the experience rather than
through their insight, that change was predominantly brought about. It is
easy to see why Max's anecdote would be unforgettable, even though he
might not be able to understand the exact way in which it was significant
for him at the time.

MAX Going off on an expedition was the absolute thing that changed my
life. I've mentioned art and education already. They were very important, but it was the expedition that was the most rewarding and
enriching experience that I had ever had.

On my last expedition something very important happened to me.
We were half-way up Scafell in October and it was really cold. We
camped when it got dark. I was the team leader, with two other kids
in the tent. My friend Jerry said, 'You don't want to put your tent
there . . .' I told him, 'Don't tell me where to pitch a tent. I've been
on three expeditions you know.' And I did pitch it there. He'd worked
out where the wind was coming from, but I ignored him.

Sure enough, in the middle of the night – it was very frightening,
half-way up this mountain, just in a sleeping bag with these other
characters around you, though luckily three or four of them were
adults – anyway, in the middle of the night, our flysheet came off and
that means trouble. I woke up and nudged the others in my tent and
got no response. They wouldn't move, never mind get out of the tent.

With great reluctance, I got out to retrieve the flysheet which had
landed a few feet out into the lake. The lake wasn't enormous, but it
was big enough and it was cold and it was dark and it was deep. It
was incredibly windy and I walked towards it, but I'd made the mis-
take of not putting anything on my feet. I waded into the lake and
eventually got it back against all the odds.

It took about fifteen minutes, but I don't think I could have managed much longer. I had this sense of being completely on my own.
It was four in the morning and I was completely convinced that everyone else was completely asleep. I remember thinking, 'You bastards!',
particularly the people in my tent. I got back in, flysheet secure and
I had a great sense of achievement. One of the kids in the tent struck

his lighter and offered me a 'roll-up'. He hadn't given me a cigarette all week. We weren't supposed to smoke in the tent, but it was great. He lit a candle and just a candle warmed me up.

I remember sitting there thinking, 'There's just this bit of cotton between us and that gale out there and we're perfectly okay, perfectly safe!' It was a real turning-point for me.

The following morning, my guru, Ed Tilman, came over to me and said, 'Well done!' as he served up his famous porridge. 'Well done, last night!'

'What do you mean?' I asked.

'I was watching you last night.'

'You were watching me? Why didn't you help?'

'Because I knew you could do it', he said. He had watched the whole thing!

After the initial anger, I really enjoyed the fact that he had been watching me and had allowed me to do it myself.

Members of staff had to be on the look-out for experiences that held the intrinsic potential to demonstrate the stark difference between the way the youngsters functioned and a more appropriate and satisfying way of living. Staff insight could lead to understanding and change that might otherwise be obliviously overlooked. Max's arrogance, irrespective of its source, often soured his achievements and his unthinking dismissal of Jerry's advice typified this. Ed Tilman's exceptional mountaineering experience instantly alerted him to something being wrong. However, his ability to recognise the therapeutic potential for Max, if he could rectify the problem which had originally arisen from arrogance, demonstrated his skill as a therapeutic member of staff. If anyone could turn 'tenderest taciturnity' into an active therapeutic ingredient it was he. Even more, he could turn the apparently mundane incidents of everyday life into psychotherapy too, and it was that which made him a effective member of staff.

Life at Peper Harow was, of course, designed to provide more than one kind of activity through which change could be generated. The immense change in so many youngsters that Table 1 (Chapter 3, p. 58) reveals arose from a process of change involving many different kinds of experience whose joint effect increased with time.

The challenge of insight which such incidents generated began early, for as people began to settle in, so their problems began to emerge more clearly.

SPENCER At first it seemed that everything would be OK and that I would fit in and get quite a lot out of it. That changed quite a lot. For a long time I didn't feel that I fitted in with the regime. At the time there was a lot of outdoor activities, canoeing, walking, climbing. I had no experience of those things and I felt very left out. I didn't want to be involved in it.

The reasons for Spencer's sense of alienation lay in his earliest childhood. He needed to resolve some of his fundamental feeling that he was unlovable and worthless, before he could feel entitled to a place among his peers. Perhaps this is why Spencer felt that the change process within him derived most significantly from the nurture of Ree, his special member of staff.

SPENCER It was much later on in my time that I started to have a bit more confidence and self-respect and belief in myself. I suppose it was through being encouraged by people like Ree. I started to feel a lot better as my time went by. I got more confident and felt more hopeful. It's difficult to point at any particular turning-point.

When Spencer resists peer-group pressure to join them in unfamiliar activities, he fails to recognise his peers' insight and concern for him. Spencer's peers certainly realised that his psychopathological sense of alienation was potentially disastrous and that overcoming any resistance to participation was central to success at Peper Harow.

Arthur was able to appreciate his peers during an earlier stage of his stay at Peper Harow and he acknowledges their interaction with him as a highly significant agent of change.

ARTHUR My attitude certainly changed over time. The bedroom that I was in from the first year was with Henry and Rupert . . . It was the most stable and secure room where you could discuss anything, no problem. Then I moved to a room over the library, where I was the senior member of the room. A lot of the reason for that was that I just knew exactly what was required from my experience with Henry and Rupert. Ralph spent his first year in there as well. He had a good deal off me. I looked after him. How comfortable people were at night was very important.

Arthur's comments also demonstrate how the culture was carried from generation to generation. It also reminds us that personality is as much nourished by practising the capacity to give as to receive. The ability to generalise positive experience into all areas of emotional life is a sign of real growth. Arthur also realises that it would not have been helpful for a resident to have got on only with his peers, or only with his individual member of staff.

ARTHUR After six months I realised that unless I sorted out my relationship with Des O'Neil, my guru, there was no way I was going to

achieve anything at all. I did it and then my relationship with him was
in the same realm as the security of that bedroom.

In Table 3 (Chapter 3, p.61) some features are shown that contain
inherent contradictions. For instance, 71 per cent of the ex-residents are
clear that relationships with either peers, staff, or usually both, improved
during their stay at Peper Harow. Although staff comments in the ex-residents' files suggest that this improvement is an under-estimate, 29 per cent
of the transcripts themselves indicate that there was no improvement. Any
significant denial of change hardly seems sustainable in the light of the
overall changes recorded in Table 1 (Chapter 3, p. 58). Perhaps the dis-
crepancy indicates that the ex-residents' feelings at the time of the research
interviews are themselves a variable. In Bernie's case, for example, when
the interview took place he was struggling with many difficulties in his
current life. Nevertheless, Bernie attempts to balance his awareness, on the
one hand, that Peper Harow offered him essential benefits, even if his feelings at the research interview were founded on Peper Harow's apparent
failure to recognise what he now feels were his most serious problems.

> BERNIE Peper Harow was a very important place. It didn't meet all my
> needs but was doing the best it could at the time . . . Peper Harow
> didn't get me anywhere near understanding what my life was actually
> like . . . It did some of the early spade-work, but I've had to do a lot
> of digging since!

Those who knew Bernie well would recognise the truth in both of his
assertions. However, when seriously stressed by today's issues, Bernie might
well even undervalue his own achievements and the courage these had
required. When he left, staff were certainly aware that Bernie, like all the
other ex-residents, still had many problems to resolve, but they were also
clear that he had changed enormously. His continual efforts since to grapple
with his problems and to develop his education is evidence of this change, for
he had few aspirations and little self-awareness when he first came.

From the many descriptions of relationships in bedroom groups, in
educational and therapeutic groups and from the several statements about
friendships that continue to exist many years later, it is obvious that peer
relationships were extremely important.

We have already gathered from Arthur that the maturation of his role in
the bedroom context derived from what he learned from his peers. The
peer group was probably the foremost culture carrier, once that culture
had initially been established. Learning a musical instrument, contributing
to discussion in a therapy group, being involved in education – all aspects

of life in the Community – were hugely influenced by the example of the majority of older residents. And yet the ex-residents' descriptions of peer behaviour are often redolent with delinquent attitudes that could be expected to reinforce resistance to change rather than to promote growth. In an attempt to be quite sure that a hidden culture did not exist at Peper Harow, perhaps the research interview over-investigated its enquiry about negative behaviour. Perhaps if matching questions about specifically positive behaviour had been asked, a greater proportion of comments such as Ralph's would have been made.

> RALPH The ability [of the peer group] to care and understand things was really phenomenal. You would see someone throw an absolute tantrum and half an hour later, they would be sitting talking about someone else's harrowing experience and offering advice.

As Ralph's comment implies, positive self-esteem could build up. The individual did not have to start their laborious uphill journey anew after every collapse.

The participants' ability to relate to others is not only demonstrated by the 71 per cent of the research participants who did say that their relationships with peers and adults improved while they were at Peper Harow. As we saw earlier, (Chapter 2, pp. 22–24), education could not have been so remarkably successful at Peper Harow unless this change had taken place.

Ben emphasises how important the different motivating effect was of the peer group at Peper Harow, compared with his previous experience at school.

> BEN I couldn't handle school, probably because of what was going on at home. I would just sit there and not listen. At school, if you got behind you felt you weren't up to scratch. Every lesson was torture. You really did feel lonely. At Peper Harow you had to want to do it, which made a massive difference. You would see other people doing well and think, 'I should be doing that.' You felt you wanted to be involved in it.

As well as the peer group, the other factor that made the difference, once again, was the outstanding staff group.

> EDMUND I did quite a lot educationally. They were brilliant teachers. The speed we got through the syllabus was amazing and a lot of that was due to the teachers. The smallness of the groups helped as well. The effort that the members of staff put into it, looking back on it, was amazing.

Most staff were qualified teachers, but everyone had to participate in the teaching programme, as well as practising as therapists and as residential childcare workers. There were nineteen staff including the director. In order to be able to offer 'A' levels in approximately twenty subjects, as well as basic and remedial teaching, this emphasis on teaching qualifications was essential. This breadth of subject provision gave us a real opportunity to begin a youngster's educational growth from whatever had actually caught his or her interest. The technology of grammar, or number, could come later, when the youngsters recognised that they absolutely needed such tools to further their real interests. However, the educational task was not simply an academic one (Chapter 2, pp. 22–24). Edmund reminds us that success depended on psychosocial change.

> EDMUND I also had to relate to other members of staff who I didn't really know, who were going to teach me. I was pretty objectionable a lot of the time. I was moody and sullen. I had to move on from that to have relationships with the staff who were going to teach me.

Because teaching staff were equally involved with the Community's psychotherapeutic objectives, issues about relationships and personal behaviour that arose in lesson situations were not simply regarded as irritating disruptions. The lesson situation was also recognised as yet another opportunity for the therapeutic application of nurture and containment and as another opportunity to support the individual struggles for self-management.

However, even though the psychological foundation of each individual's life was always regarded as the priority, it is evident that the specific educational goals were not diluted. Of the research sample, 79 per cent engaged with formal education, 77 per cent of them obtaining formal GCE qualifications. As we see in Table 1 (Chapter 3, p. 58), 82 per cent had previously demonstrated their inability to apply themselves age-appropriately to schoolwork before they came. Some simply could not concentrate, others were so disruptive that they had been expelled and others had truanted for most of the time.

When youngsters arrived at Peper Harow, there was usually an initial period of improved behaviour. But as they became aware of other people's problems, they rapidly discovered that their own had not been left behind. So their habitual behavioural responses rapidly returned. In the face of their aggressive and disruptive behaviour, normal education was impossible. We have already seen that a period of apparent dormancy was an essential precursor. It was actually a period during which phased preparation for formal learning could take place. Time was required to allow the frozen emotional and intellectual learning processes to germinate. However, reference has already been made to the language development of the first two years which considerably increased the ability to learn (Chapter 2, pp. 23–24). If, as Clare Winnicott suggests (Winnicott 1968), trauma and deprivation rob children's language of its emotional significance, the youngsters' desperate wish to become an accepted part of the peer group was itself a major stimulant of significant communication in their language once more. To become accepted, they had to understand whatever issue the peer group was caught up in. Whether this was a style of pop music, or a shouting match in the morning Community Meeting, they had to be able to contribute to discussion and they could not avoid listening to it.

Many youngsters were delighted when they arrived to be told that they were not allowed to attend lessons. This was hardly a sophisticated psychological strategy, but it dramatically reduced their habitual antagonism towards learning. There being no battle with authority to be had, it became easier to be open to what was going on around them. In lieu of other influences, they were bound to take on peer-group values.

> EDMUND I really wanted to do lessons, because everybody else was doing it. But there was another feeling of 'I don't want to do lessons.' Not having to do lessons was one of the things that attracted me to Peper Harow in the first place. But it came to the point where I felt that I had to learn something, or I would be ignorant for ever. I suppose my education was linked to my emotions. It was just a progression really.

There was a smaller group who were troubled by this embargo on education. For them, working virtuously at lessons, irrespective of the outcome, would at least have been a reassuring statement that they were not as different from their peers outside Peper Harow as they actually were. Some may well have felt more comfortable buried in ostensibly profitable activity than in coming to terms with the reality of their behaviour and with the painful feelings that promoted it. Thus a scholastic sabbatical was not so easily acceptable to everyone. Suggesting that emotional problems needed prior resolution was like a red rag to some youngsters, as Roy's dismissive comments imply.

> ROY Education should have started earlier. If they had school from day one, I would've hated it, but I needed it. I liked the way that they did education when they did it, but I think that it should've been done after two or three months. Those are important years that you spent at Peper Harow, and we were learning about psychotherapeutic theories, rather than how to use a computer, how to drive a car, or how to use a shovel.

In fact, premature involvement in formal education might not only have reinforced their history of educational failure, it might also have reinforced their overall defensiveness. Yet it seemed more likely that, once their emotional problems were somewhat calmed, it was clear that they would be able to apply themselves wholeheartedly.

> ARTHUR Education and emotion were obviously connected in that they weren't going to allow you to do it if you weren't capable of making the commitment.

Not surprisingly, it took some youngsters longer than others to be able to tolerate the anxiety generated by the lesson scenario. Youngsters whose experience of adults had always been negative or unfulfilling inevitably felt vulnerable before adult authority. Of course, their behaviour needed to be manageable if lessons were not to be wrecked. The gap between the youngster's intellectual potential and their ability to apply themselves to serious study tended to undermine their fragile self-belief, and it had to be bridged.

> HENRY When people felt better about themselves, they felt more confident educationally . . . Years of work can be thrown away in a day. Some people are very wary about exposing themselves to failure in that way.

Although some people took longer than others to become able to study appropriately, a surprisingly large proportion of the sample – 62 per cent – insightfully recognised the link between their emotional condition and beginning and managing formal education. Twenty-three per cent were not able to acknowledge the specific connection and a further 15 per cent denied a connection. It is likely that this continued denial may relate to an individual's current ability to acknowledge the full significance of what they actually received from Peper Harow. Yet even those who are not sure about the link between emotional growth and educational attainment still engaged with education at Peper Harow, and a third of them also went on to tertiary education.

Hamish's improvement in self-image helped to free his motivation and he certainly represents the majority whose experience supports the view that:

> HAMISH there was a link between my education and my emotional development. My ability to cope with my own feelings enabled me to take on more education. Possibly the education enabled me to do well in the Community because the discipline of learning was beneficial.

The transcripts express almost uniform enthusiasm about the use of the grounds, the studios and expeditions and camps. Staff became extremely skilled in initiating play activities while camouflaging their own input. They especially understood how critical the need to play was, if these same adolescents/infants were eventually to engage with examination work.

A major advantage of the residential situation was that it enabled each individual's emotional problems to be addressed whenever the opportunity arose and whatever they were actually doing. For instance, examination qualifications were as essential to the Peper Harow residents' future as to that of any other teenager. Yet, at the same time as the syllabus was being focused on, the teacher would be actively thinking about the way each day's achievement could strengthen an individual's capacity to receive emotional nurture, which, in turn, would enhance his or her capacity for relationships. There were many socio-educational benefits of camps and expeditions as well as many opportunities for re-experiencing growthful qualities of play that had been missed in childhood.

And the staff, too, came to recognise that the need for play and the need for persistent academic effort over time were equally essential psychotherapeutic ingredients. Work and play were two facets of creativity that were generated by a sense of personal value and they also helped to feed the very sense of worth that motivated them. Erikson's model of psychosocial development sees the industriousness that should be a feature of the period of life he calls School Age as a direct reformulation of the imaginative and creative processes that are encouraged in the preceding Play Age. But the ability to play in the first place derives from an established sense of self – what Erikson calls a sense of autonomy – and in the normal course of events this derives from the initial explorations of Infancy, encouraged in manifold ways by a confident and successful mother.

The member of staff's task was to integrate these many factors. Most staff were teachers whose basic training had not emphasised that education is also a psychosocial developmental process. Thus, initially, they did not recognise that reinvigorating normal development was also a psychotherapeutic process. However, as teachers, they were certainly familiar with a notion of sequential development and of the need to organise their teaching so that a student was only faced with what he or she had been enabled to cope with beforehand. The youngster's relationship with his or her guru was primarily supposed to be a therapeutically integrating one. It had many parallels with the fortunate infant's relationship with his or her mother. The mother too fulfils a wide variety of tasks as a result of her nurturing, reassuring, physically and personally supporting and stimulating activities. She looks after the baby, plays with and stimulates him or her to new explorations. She lays down the foundations of independent identity and accepts responsibility for maintaining boundaries that he or she is too young to manage personally. Within the individual's relationship with his or her guru was a re-enactment of similar experiences, while the pedagogic aspect of the relationship focused on ensuring that growth did occur. Education therefore was conducted at depth. It was rooted at last within a parental kind of relationship while at the same time it was designed to feel like a reassuringly shared task with mutual engagement.

> VERONICA Barbara and I talked about education in our weekly sessions until I decided to do it. I did music and maths and I loved doing maths. I did them with Barbara Sanderson. She was my guru. I wouldn't have done those things without Barbs.

Henry emphasises the need for play. His use of the word 'space' demonstrates not only its literal meaning but also that play's metaphoric exploration of self and one's environment – which had so often been missed in these youngsters' Early Childhood – could become developmentally significant once more.

> HENRY What was important was that it was 'space' to grow up. It was important that people could have the 'space' to play childish games. There was a guy called Terry, who used to be into tanks and guns. He had a whole battlefield like you'd expect a little boy of five or six to have and this was a sixteen- or seventeen-year-old, living the life that he never really did when he was younger.

But as well as regressing and finding meaning in developmentally earlier kinds of play activity, there also needed to be simultaneous opportunities for enjoyment that was socially appropriate to adolescence. Whatever the form of the activity, it was important that it should not reinforce a youngster's erstwhile delinquent image. The 'space' at Peper Harow engendered many experiences that were intrinsically rather than artificially joyful and exciting.

> HAROLD It was important to me. There was the swimming pool, gym, river . . . I was between fourteen and sixteen and it was just wonderful.

Peper Harow's special architecture and long history gave it a real identity. It had not been deliberately built to be indistinguishable from other houses on a housing estate. Its appropriateness for its task actually lay in its difference. Roy's excitement in describing the building is aroused by its very individuality.

ROY I loved the environment, climbing trees and jumping in the river and exploring the countryside around. That was the best bit of it. My first impressions of the place were of how nice it was and how nice the furniture was. It was an interesting house. There were loads of nooks and crannies and loads of character.

Spencer eloquently describes the huge contrast that existed for those whose material background was as deprived as their emotional world. 'Political correctness' since the 1960s has only seemed able to perceive large estates in the country as an alienating disadvantage for such young people. Peper Harow demonstrated that an initially incomprehensible and unfamiliar lifestyle can awaken fresh perceptions for disturbed and deprived youngsters.

SPENCER I remember where I was brought up on Dogberry Road. As you walk up from Najera Square, on the right-hand side there were dark Victorian flats and the other side was the same. All I remember is that there was no clean linen and there was a yard with big council dustbins. Nowhere to play, no bathroom, no hot water. So from there to the total opposite of Peper Harow with the beautiful grounds and trees and landscapes and beautiful air and feeling of freedom . . . it was the best thing in the world. For me it was really significant.

If relating to people or to a serious programme of study was still too threatening, exploring the estate provided a temporary alternative kind of relationship especially for newcomers. The exceptionally beautiful park generated enormous enthusiasm from the youngsters, but sometimes it also put them in touch with sadness.

SPENCER I would walk around the grounds, sometimes in deep melancholy and I would have a good cry. I'd really sort of cleansed myself and those grounds were my salvation and my sanctuary.

Spencer, like several others, needed to express grief, even if he could not initially share his sense of emptiness and loss. He needed somewhere that enabled his depression and sadness to well into consciousness. The residents' emotional disturbance also expressed itself on camps and expeditions, though the less familiar environment of a mountainside underlined inappropriate behaviour and the urgent need for change.

RALPH I can remember being on a cycling camp and coming round a mountain on the wrong side of the road and seeing a blue minivan. I thought, 'Oh shit!' I had had a tantrum earlier in the day and ended up rolling down the hill wrapped up in the bike.

Ralph clearly recognises the link between his disturbed emotional world – his 'tantrum earlier in the day' – and his so-called 'accident', brought about by his cycling on the wrong side of a 'blind' mountain road!

Edmund not only found it difficult to relate to adult teachers, but equally to participate appropriately with his peers, which is why he avoided team sports. Fortunately, a variety of activities were available to ensure that the psychosocial development engendered by peers that Edmund and others needed was available, if not in one form then in another.

> EDMUND I didn't get involved with sports. I found it very difficult to get involved with anything to do with teams. The expeditions were really good. I wish I'd done more of that.

Some issues in the course of camp or expedition activity, just as at Peper Harow itself, might appear to require the staff's and the peer group's unequivocal disciplinary capacity.

> RALPH There was one sailing camp where Ranji and Harold had a bit of a fight. The next thing, Ranji walks into the tent with an axe! It took three of us to pull them apart!

Despite the opportunity which outdoor activities provided for the manifestation of emotionally disturbed behaviour, 82 per cent of the ex-residents also record many pleasurable memories of these adventurous occasions. To hold a fund of good memories within one and to be able to recall them with appreciation is, of course, yet another indication of current healthy psychological functioning.

As we have seen, there were therapeutic and developmental advantages to be derived from members of staff who could function as skilled teachers, or as psychotherapeutic social workers, or in their several other roles. As a result, what the youngsters consistently encountered was staff concern and insight. This contrasted significantly with their previous assumptions about adults and, therefore, about what kinds of adults they too might become. Not only did their new kind of relationship with an adult begin to ease the pain they carried within them, but it also stimulated a real optimism towards their future.

This did not happen easily, of course, for at the same time the youngsters' emotional deprivation contradictorily seemed to have left them impervious to emotional nourishment. Despite the caring attention of exceptional individuals, the youngsters' response remained inhibited. For them, it appeared that nothing less than the integration of as many good experiences as Peper Harow could devise could be enough to erode their apprehensive resistance. Similar resistance seemed to be expressed towards the symbolic house itself. In the same way as a mother communicates with her baby through a variety of physical and material forms, which reinforce the baby's belief that he or she is loved and is therefore worthwhile, so we hoped that the positive messages deriving from the variety of everyday experiences would mutually reinforce the youngsters' emerging sense of significance and value.

The material environment and lifestyle at Peper Harow were full of such personally enhancing potential and this is acknowledged by 79 per cent of the transcripts. Nevertheless, individual responses to different parts of the environment often reveal more about the individual than about the actual quality of food, or bathrooms, or anything else.

> MAX The thing that was a landmark for me was when they put in the new showers. Individual toilets with locks at last, so you had some privacy – fantastic. You felt looked after on some primary level that hadn't existed before.

Some ex-residents were able to bask in the physically pleasurable experiences.

> SAM It was very nice having a place to sit and look at the fire. It was like having a camp fire. Sometimes you couldn't see who was sitting on the other side of the fire, you were just sitting talking into the fire. We used cedar wood. It smelt nice and it felt nice to come in wet and stand in front of the fire, so you could dry yourself off and then scarper off over the carpet upstairs.

Others found it much more difficult to know how to enjoy their surroundings, as though they simply lacked the capacity.

> EDMUND There was too much emphasis on cleaning things all the time. It did make some people feel good, but it really wound other people up. It didn't feel like home at all. But I didn't know what home was, particularly.

Learning to enjoy the environment often seemed to be fraught with the same difficulty as relating to staff and peers. The gulf between wanting to be loved, yet feeling threatened even while recognising the genuineness of caring that existed, sometimes seemed insurmountable. Love had been craved in childhood, but reaching out for it had always ended in disappointment. At Peper Harow, the residents still wanted to be loved, but for a long time they still hoped that somehow it would be found within their family. To accept that the Community was more likely to meet their

needs seemed to imply that they would finally have to give up their unre-
quited longing for a normal childhood and, despite Peper Harow, remain
forever unsatisfied. This made accepting the Community's symbols of care
and its assumption of its residents' intrinsic worth, especially difficult.

One of the areas that produced most resistance was in the preparation
and consumption of food. However, if the youngsters' reactions to food
demonstrated something about their initial relationships with mother and
with the sequence of all that occurred in their life thereafter, the residential setting could itself provide a new opportunity to exchange
long-established attitudes that were immensely influenced by poor early
nurturing for more personally enhancing ones. This was the main reason
for making the residents engage with cooking for each other instead of
having professional cooks, as in most institutions, and also for the redesign
of the whole kitchen and dining areas. Yet everything to do with food
provoked resistance as well as appreciation.

> ROY The food was good. I enjoyed the cooking and I liked the fact that
> there was always fruit out and bread and you didn't have to ask
> anyone for it. I used to see people turn up there ill and thin and after
> a while they would be healthy, good-looking people. They would have
> a glow about them.

However, Roy may be deliberately ignoring the symbolic significance of
food, finding its gastronomic quality easier to cope with. His enthusiasm
certainly contrasts with Ralph's tearful Feast.

> RALPH My first Feast was at Christmas. I ate the melon and cried for
> the rest of the meal. I couldn't accept any of it. The Feasts were very
> important. They were the hardest times for a lot of people to accept –
> all this abundance!

One of the most difficult problems was to provide fresh milk. Though
it could be consumed in huge quantities, especially at times of raised
stress, it was deliberately contaminated and turned into a sour disappointment whenever possible.

> ARTHUR The old kitchens were quite a story. They had milk in churns
> with all sorts of alien objects floating in it. When I first went there it
> was quite barbaric: 'Comme la guerre!' as the French say.

The destructive symbolism seemed obvious. Our problem was to enable
something constructive to be expressed in place of endless destruction.
Several youngsters, however, preferred the 'barbaric times'. After all, the
'alien objects' did not enter the churns without help!

The giving and receiving of food must be one of the most important ways through which an infant begins to establish a sense of personal worth. Peper Harow residents had rarely enjoyed the good fortune of such an idyllic relationship with their mothers, so it was hardly surprising that emotional exchange between them and others was often so difficult.

Each resident was regularly obliged to prepare the day's meals with another resident. To ensure the outcome, staff would sometimes help, but there were no cooks and cleaners. Our prior objective each mealtime was a therapeutic one, and this was sometimes recognised.

> SPENCER The food was terrific. I have never eaten so healthily since . . . The psychology that went into that was spot on, certainly for me. The fact that we had to cook was good, despite no one wanting to do it. Some lovely things would happen over the day with the people you were cooking with and with members of staff.

As with everything else, 'lovely things' were the growthful side of the mixed experience which the daily food provision promoted. Like the appalling behaviour that occasionally contrasted with the fun and growth of camps, food sometimes generated unresolved pathology, perhaps through symbolic behaviour.

> MAX Food was enormously important. Even though there was so much, people would still steal food . . . All you had to do was ask.

The significant question, therefore, was why someone would rather steal their food than receive it from someone else. On one occasion Max was himself caught stealing a tin of biscuits. A member of staff watched the theft proceed and at the last moment, stepped in with a grin and removed the tin from an open-mouthed Max. His timing appealed to Max's adolescent humour. His non-recriminatory method of re-establishing appropriate behaviour, was redolent of how a parent might say 'No!' to a similar action from a toddler.

Some people might wonder how Max would learn right from wrong without condemnation of the behaviour being expressed by the adult. However, Max already knew he was doing something wrong. He knew that he could not simply walk out of the food store with the tin, which was why he was lowering it on a rope through a window to his accomplice. The member of staff's task was to enable the contradiction between knowledge and behaviour to raise its own questions within Max about his desire to steal rather than to receive rightfully what he would like. If Max's focus was to be kept on that message, his delinquent defensiveness needed to be kept at bay. Re-establishing a boundary, albeit accompanied by humour, achieved that focus. Max's memory of the lesson confirms its effectiveness. Anger and retribution would merely have reinforced his delinquent hostility.

In evaluating how to respond to behaviour, staff had to assess what element of a situation was actually normal behaviour for any adolescent and what proportion, therefore, related to the individual's emotional disturbance, which called for a more considered response.

> HENRY The environment became more plush after a few years. The kitchens were really gross when we first got there. Milk came out of a big churn with flies and stuff floating in it. It was foul.
>
> It felt that some of the early magic was lost when everywhere became carpeted. When it was basic it felt like we were all in the same challenge together. When it became extremely comfortable it felt weird. Some people found it extremely difficult.

Henry's difficulty in appreciating the material development of the Community was of a piece with Ralph's difficulty in accepting the Feast. At the same time, what Henry describes as both 'foul' and 'basic', also has an adolescent flavour to it. Functioning as an uncouth adolescent and shocking adults with nonconformist attitudes and behaviour still required room for expression, even if so much rehabilitative work on earlier developmental phases was essential. Where the line should be drawn was inevitably an ongoing debate.

The bedrooms were an area of the house where greater individuality of expression seemed possible. The individual's own bedspace allowed this most of all. Typically, adolescent bedrooms were often a total mess, or perhaps they would be decorated by their inhabitants according to some fiendishly idiosyncratic design, though these were often astonishingly creative.

> HENRY Once you were in your own room and the lights went down, it was a different world. You would have great conversations. Some of the most memorable things went on when it was purely our environment.

Henry had been in institutions for most of his life. He would obviously value privacy, especially when he had really begun to believe that he was entitled to life on his terms.

> HENRY The bedrooms were real dens of iniquity. You had your own bedspace and it was something that no one else had any influence over. That was important.

Those who had grown up with the Community found its anti-establishment presentation and its robbers' den environment safe and unthreatening. Changing that atmosphere was bound to be threatening. Not surprisingly, change was always resisted initially at Peper Harow. It seems to be an inevitable stage in the recovery from emotional injury. Spontaneous enthusiasm was reserved for what the youngsters were already in tune with, even if this was delinquent.

The extent to which youngsters would misuse their independence to reinforce their resistance to change was obviously a concern. Yet although this did occur occasionally, privacy was generally used responsibly. Staff had to trust and accept a measure of abuse of that trust, just like most parents. Testing boundaries eventually helps adolescents to establish their own positive values. Unlike most parents, however, the residential situation and the therapeutic demand for openness placed a greater strain on staff at Peper Harow. When staff knew that the youngsters were abusing their bedroom independence, the real challenge was to gauge how much restraint they should apply to their adult impulse to intervene.

Predominantly, however, despite the difficulties which the environmental changes aroused for some youngsters, their response was positive and great care of the new furnishings showed that it was appreciated.

SOLLY I was there when Peper Harow changed from an old dark shell of a building into something warm and lush and comfortable. It was really nice to sit around in those chairs, just laze around and feel really, really comfortable. I think the environment was really beneficial. Just making you feel very calm.

The object, of course, was not to spend money for the sake of doing so. We were trying to create an environment that might well bring underlying resistance to nurture into the open. It may well be that the preference for the 'rough and tough' past demonstrates an awareness of the challenge to those neurotic unconscious attitudes that needed addressing.

The real question is whether or not the experiences of everyday life have an effect upon our unconscious inner life. If, as Freud suggests (Freud 1938), our responses to the events of everyday life reflect our unconscious feelings, in the form of slips of the tongue and jokes, it becomes obvious that certain environments will arouse certain kinds of response, themselves capable of illuminating hitherto unconscious attitudes.

ERIC A fortune was spent on the eating area and there was massive building works. I thought that it was a bit over the top with those really expensive tables. I wasn't complaining, but I felt that the money could've been better spent. It made a nice environment, no doubt about that. Maybe other kids did need that, but I didn't at the time.

If an environment can be designed so as to arouse unconscious feelings, it should be possible to ensure that it also gives those who live there some experience of feeling good about themselves. Thus it would offer potential nurture, which would be especially important for those who had been emotionally deprived in early life and who would be exceptionally resistant to more overt nurture. Sometimes the huge investment of thought and money into the physical environment was misunderstood. It was supposed that the object was in some way to balance the material inadequacy of the youngsters' past lives by material excess. This would have been a naive attempt at compensation, whereas the real intention was to ensure that the actual material environment as well as the 'climate' that derived from the interpersonal relationships would both contribute in their manifold ways to the psychotherapeutic process.

The advantage of the twenty-four-hour residential experience lies in its potential to turn all experiences into nurturing and resolving ones. Thus our objectives were to find ways to enhance the environment's potential for this, just as much as with the daily programme or with the style of relationships. The grounds had to be developed so as to encourage exploration and play, the bedrooms a sense of security and ownership, the lavatories and bathrooms something that was redolent of personal physical respect, and the whole eating process to provide a sense of deep pleasure, reliability and sufficiency, despite many individuals' long-established propensity towards paranoid suspicion and rejection. These objectives were made more difficult by Peper Harow's grand Palladian architecture. Nevertheless, the residents' group had the capacity to deny the intrinsic worth of anything that challenged their unconscious defences.

The youngsters' resistance to insight and change cannot be over-estimated. During their years of wretchedness they had become increasingly despairing of any change, other than for the worse. Thus we have seen that their first contact with Peper Harow often came as a shock. The difference between their previous history of increasingly self-destructive and anti-social behaviour and the new way that staff and youngsters related, the values they acknowledged and the environment in which they lived, was undeniable. The new youngster was absolutely compelled to stop and consider this strange place. That very step was the first towards a changed way of life. Becoming caught up in the social imperatives – having to clean, to cook, to look after the general fabric – carried the individual further away from their endless, negative functioning and, although they would continually wish to resist, the peer pressure that patently aroused the desire to become part of the group became irresistible. Several transcripts describe recalcitrant new members of the Community continually having to be brought back to finish their cooking or cleaning chores. That this housekeeping system worked at all was because the peer group appreciated its worth and not, as is so often the case, because of adult imposition.

> BEN It became clearer the longer you were there, how important it was to have that decor and to respect that . . . Saturday was the time when we'd let our hair down. We'd clean up the house first thing in the morning. Everybody would help out and we'd all have radios tuned to the same station. I've never had quite so much fun as cleaning that place.

However, after a year or two, once the youngster really felt part of this lifestyle, he or she would even begin to practise their new maturity by encouraging newer youngsters to take on the social values of the group. Perhaps they would take a junior role in someone's initial interview for the first time, or perhaps they would begin to discuss starting lessons, or start to learn to play an instrument. They might start to make their first interventions in the Community Meeting.

> HENRY At first you sat there, bored and silent and wishing you were somewhere else. Then gradually, you began to take an interest. When you began to accept that Peper Harow was important to you, you started contributing on a community basis.

As participation developed, so the daily experiences began to effect psychological change. However, we still felt that formal psychotherapeutic intervention was necessary. The experiences of many youngsters had been so traumatising and deprivatory, and from such an early age, that leaving the development of insight to chance felt too risky. Unless psychological change was carefully managed their past experiences would continue to fester, even if their current surroundings effected a measure of functional improvement.

Even the Approved School, with its different view of the purpose of discipline and despite its sub-culture of abuse and bullying and its delinquent camaraderie, could still provide a sense of group identity. In response to its structure and certainty, youngsters' behaviour in Approved Schools almost always improved – while they remained in the institution.

BERNIE When you've lived in poverty with no sheets on your bed and no change of clothes, the *Approved School* was a luxury! It was luxury to have three meals a day. A profound thing that happened at Approved School was that we got breakfast in the morning, which had never been part of my life before.

However, once youngsters left such establishments without any change within them and without the external support of the school, their behaviour inevitably deteriorated once more. Unfortunately, as Redl and Wineman (1951) emphasise, their apparent change in response to the generally increased experience of structure and certainty could only be a final, though an especially powerful, defence against real change. The real and permanent establishment of a creative and growing personality requires the springs of an individual's functioning to be restored. This requires change from within, rather than conformity to other people's values.

This above all, is why at Peper Harow – despite recognising the paradox that most youngsters would resist the very psychotherapeutic experience that they needed – we still hoped that through the variety of such experiences, whether as traditional psychotherapy or in the form of activities in the grounds or on a mountainside, a youngster would begin to re-establish him or herself from within. We saw the Large Daily Group, the Weekly Small Group and individual work with their guru as being central psychotherapeutic features.

Perhaps he or she would be able to make use of their individual relationship with their guru. New members of staff were usually responsible for new residents. Their main task was to spend time together establishing a good relationship. As this grew so their initial friendship could become more therapeutically sophisticated, especially as clinical supervision became established.

EDMUND I had individual sessions with my guru. We would sit down and chat for about an hour. Luke Pearson was my guru to start with and then Jack Weaver. The sessions were very useful, especially during the last few years. They were like role models and someone you could chat to. The only person you could really chat to was your guru. They were the counsellors really. It was an important relationship.

They may also have developed a psychotherapeutic relationship with their Small Group.

SPENCER I was in the Friday group. It was a good experience even though it was painful. There were times when it had an incredibly

85

close and intimate feeling and people felt safe enough to talk about the things that terrified them.

Quite often a lot of the stuff that happened in the Friday group would be fed back into the whole meeting. That was quite positive. A lot of positive things came from it.

Spencer's comment again emphasises the interactive and potentially mutually reinforcing aspect of Peper Harow's activities. Perhaps it was this that made formal psychotherapy especially effective in the residential setting.

MAX I was in the Wednesday Small Group . . . It was really important and I almost never missed it. There was none of this confidentiality. We all used to discuss what the groups were like and what happened in them.

Even if the Small Groups were run down or slagged off, there was always something important happening in them and they were very much an anchor for lots of people, even if they would resist going to them like mad.

Or perhaps they would become psychologically engaged in the powerful Large Group emotion of the daily Community Meeting.

BEN Although my input was virtually zero, the Community Meeting was the most important. I think that I would've got a lot more out of it if I had been prepared to contribute to it, but you couldn't go into that room and not get anything out of it.

Everyone had to come to the daily Community Meeting, which lasted for an hour. Despite Ben's comments, they frequently represented stress and resistance rather than change. Everyone also had to attend their Small Group which lasted for an hour and a half per week. These too were viewed with ambivalence by many residents.

VERA I was in the Thursday afternoon's group. I don't remember getting anything important out of it. I liked it better than the Community Meetings, maybe because it was smaller. Even if you didn't say anything yourself, more things came out. I got more out of them than I ever did out of the Community Meetings.

The guru was expected to provide the ongoing evaluation reports and records for consideration in the regular reviews that occurred throughout the youngster's stay. They would also expect to meet the youngster on his or her own for at least one hour every week. In order to develop a maximally fruitful relationship, they would probably have to spend more time than this together. Their work as a guru was also regularly supervised by consultants and by senior staff. In Peper Harow's beginning an attempt was made to reduce threat by jokingly calling this personal member of staff the youngster's 'guru' – a term that, at the time, conjured up bearded Eastern sages who ministered to certain pop stars. The professional nomenclature of key workers and care workers and case workers and therapists may emphasise the sophistication of their task, but it also arouses adolescent suspicions about the power and sincerity of adults. The guru joke lasted so long that eventually both new residents and staff forgot that its original introduction had not been wholly serious.

> MAX I had a very tenuous relationship with my guru, but he did stick by me for four-and-a-half years. He didn't shirk the job, which couldn't have been easy. I remember that he was almost euphoric when I got into college. He was almost in tears, beside himself with joy.

Max is more enthusiastic about his relationship with his Small Group than with his guru. Yet to the onlooker, his relationship with Ed Tilman seemed enormously important. It often seemed that Max did everything he could to be rejected, but Ed maintained his patient concern, just as he had done on the night of Max's adventure with the tent. Ed's consistency may well have been a critical factor in Max's survival at Peper Harow.

Ben had a more open commitment to Vincent Morley, his guru. Vince's style was not uncommon among staff at Peper Harow.

> BEN Vince was really laid back and I didn't even think about it. When we had a guru talk every week, I didn't even think that it was part of the healing process and didn't feel that he was trying to 'therap' me. We would just talk and there would always be something to talk about. Maybe we would just go and walk around the grounds, but the things we talked about were what had happened, how we felt about being there, relationships going on. It just felt very natural and most of the staff were like that.

Albert acknowledges that much of his ability to keep his relationship going with his children must be due to the strength of his partner, Val. However, one is drawn to speculate, from what Albert says about his guru Celia Wentworth, how much of this also derived from his relationship with her. His emotionally deprived infancy and childhood still seems only partly resolved. Nevertheless, his relationship with Celia must have contributed hugely to the emotional recovery he has made.

ALBERT My sessions with Celia Wentworth were important. I felt that there was something about Celia, something really comforting. Not like a mother, more someone to talk to. She would understand. After a while, I felt really close to her. She was always important to me.

Of all three formal psychotherapeutic interventions, the relationship with the guru, so the transcripts indicate, has had the most significance for the ex-residents. In individual psychotherapy, maintaining the resident's hope and effort were critical. Often lacking the strength to persist, the youngster was dependent on his guru being able to 'keep him at it'.

Rupert, like Ben, also conveys something of his guru's style. For the youngster, becoming dependent in therapy without surrendering his or her autonomy was essential if early development was to be reinvigorated through the one-to-one relationship. The gurus' style allowed this to become acceptable, even for adolescents who usually would find the vulnerability of dependency on another person utterly intolerable.

RUPERT There was a lot of support from the staff. I had a lot of faith in my guru, Edward Balliol. For the first time, here were adults who were on your level. They got pissed off with you as well and had a laugh and everything. You could see, even in the most delinquent moments that you weren't in a playground. This was something serious. You knew that there was a chance of sorting something out, instead of winding up in some bog in Piccadilly . . . there was always hope around. You became attached to your guru. There is a certain dependency. I used to really like going to see Edward and having a cup of tea and a Gauloise. I would sit in his flat and read his books and talk to him. I think that most people did like to go and see their gurus and have a chat. That was really important. Edward seemed like a really nice bloke, someone you could trust, with a great sense of humour. As indeed all the staff were. They were all individuals. Establishing that relationship was very important.

It was harder in some ways, to ensure that all five Small Groups and later, the New Persons' Group and the Leavers' Group too, were consistently psychotherapeutically effective. There were some residents whose resistance to sitting down for an hour was unmanageable. Few staff, especially in the early days, had received any group psychotherapy training, although four of the five Small Groups were co-conducted by experienced consultant psychiatrists. Again we had hoped that by establishing regular boundaries of time and of membership they would have developed organically.

Ninety-one per cent of the sample made comments on the Small Groups, 32 per cent of which were negative and 59 per cent were generally positive. In comparison, 65 per cent of the sample felt that the Community Meeting was generally helpful, though 35 per cent seemed to disagree. However, 79 per cent felt that their relationship with their guru was predominantly positive and only 15 per cent disagreed. These transcript percentages are supported by similar figures that are drawn from the files.

It seems fair to conclude from the various sources of information that, although one kind of therapeutic experience may have been more important for a particular individual, it was the combination of a wide variety of experiences that was responsible for the youngsters' initial attachment and growth. Of the areas that are defined as specifically psychotherapeutic influences – the environment, the peer group, the Small Group, the Large Group, education and the staff, it is the latter above all that receives the interviewees' greatest appreciation.

There is much that is encouraging in what the ex-residents say about what made for change at Peper Harow. Few remarks are simply what they seem. Some comments are accurate criticisms of the programme's inadequacy. Other comments remind the discerning reader that some psychological struggles are lifelong, even if they can be generally managed. And yet such unresolved problems can also throw their own form of light on the Peper Harow process. The next two chapters attempt to understand more fully the significance of such comments and of the ex-residents' collated opinions.

5

LIMITATIONS OF INSIGHT

The ex-residents' comments concerning their past and current life demonstrate their successful transformation. And yet, some of their comments also contradict the very success that they acknowledge. It may be that Peper Harow's treatment programme was limited for a variety of managerial reasons. In addition, effecting profound psychological change in the face of the damage which so many youngsters had suffered throughout their earlier lives presents an exceptional clinical challenge.

All organisations have to be well managed if they are to achieve their objectives but, at Peper Harow, many elements of the organisational structure also had a psychological significance which made clear-cut management objectives less straightforward. The managerial intention at Peper Harow was to establish and maintain an environment that enabled psychotherapeutic change and growth to occur. Peper Harow was never simply intended to be like a well-run boarding school, where providing enough individual attention would enable the youngster to catch up with their psychosocial, chronological development. Instead, Peper Harow, as a therapeutic Community, was supposed to be a situation in which the pressures and value judgements of normality could be suspended. It was intended to be an environment in which the potential meaning of everyday experiences actually enriched the unconscious personality of youngsters. As we have seen, the significance of that unusual psychosocial environment was emphasised by their very first encounter with the Community in their initial interview. It was designed to help the youngster think afresh about his or her behaviour and needs, and the lifestyle that they encountered on that day was intended to give them an experience of the way the Community offered emotional nurture through its environment and through its personal relationships.

From the Community's beginning, it was hoped that the meaningful environment which would eventually be developed would appear to engage spontaneously with the youngsters' unconscious processes. This largely unconscious daily relationship would itself encourage the revelation of their inner worlds, through the expression of their fantasies in their behaviour and in other forms of communication. However, because their pre-existing fantasy life was so rooted in fear, confusion and hostility, its expression inevitably led to repeated conflict between the profound misconceptions which an individual's fantasy revealed, and everyone else's everyday actuality. Therapeutically, each uncomfortable clash could also be seen as an opportunity, because self-control and insight largely derived from this continuous need to resolve the conflict.

However, to ensure that conflict was being turned to therapeutic purposes, management of the process – particularly the maintaining of the effectiveness of the process – had to be an accepted equal responsibility of both staff and the youngsters. The daily Community Meetings were predominantly concerned with managing and with making sense of the youngsters' bizarre behaviour. If an individual's behaviour was eventually to change, then whatever unconsciously concealed reasons lay beneath it had to be made manifest.

There were different ways by which this expression and clarification took place but, when it occurred in a group setting, it had an effect that was difficult to forget. Perhaps tears would express the beginning of grief that had been many years overdue. A discussion about reparation for damage or injury might reveal a new chance to relate to someone, which, in turn, might well indicate the germination of genuine concern about other people.

> BEN I remember one Community Meeting with Alf Grant. He never used to speak at meetings. He would sit in the corner and not say anything. I remember one Community Meeting where he started speaking and it all came out. After that he was a completely different person. He could talk about what he'd done and what had happened to him. It was a dramatic change.

When the united peer group set out to persuade an individual to acknowledge the reality of their behaviour and then to understand its source, that individual would then find his or her familiar forms of resistance almost impossible to maintain. Nevertheless, there seemed to be endless difficulties that could dilute the potential of the programme that had been carefully constructed to make manifest and to engage the youngsters' unconscious attitudes and feelings. The peer group itself varied in its therapeutic effectiveness for several reasons. For instance, if the director and the staff group were visibly at cross purposes, this might undermine the resident's group sense of security and self-confidence. Such disagreement reminded too many youngsters of traumatic conflicts between their own warring parents. But, however much the adults consciously tried to avoid their unresolved difficulties being expressed in front of the youngsters, the latter were supersensitively on the look-out for the slightest rift.

> SPENCER   I don't think that they were together as a staff team. M. was the driving force. He is a very charismatic bloke, with lots of very good ideas, but he could also ride roughshod over other people. I felt that there was some resentment amongst the staff. Certainly since leaving, that came out in talking to staff members. Residents were picking that up and it was being discussed at the time.

As a result, residents sometimes saw conflict where none existed while at other times they unconsciously provoked conflict in those around them. Traumatised youngsters live in fear of catastrophe. For them, anxiety is triggered by the slightest suggestion of anger or inexplicable conflict. However, Spencer is also right that there were real as well as imagined conflicts between the adults at Peper Harow. Unfortunately, this is what one would expect within any organisation. It was the extra psychopathological pressures on staff in a therapeutic community for adolescents that made the understanding and the management of conflict a continuous issue.

For instance, when conflict between staff arose from disturbed adolescent attitudes that staff had unconsciously absorbed, it took time for their feelings to be processed. Until that had occurred, disagreement within the staff group was likely. In addition, staff themselves, like many adults in their twenties and thirties, had not necessarily resolved all their own adolescent conflicts about authority and power. However, these particular adolescents' emotional problems would have affected the relationships of any staff whose therapeutic task was to engage with those problems, irrespective of how mature they were themselves.

Staff cared deeply about the youngsters' emotional suffering. Yet even that concern sometimes led towards over-identification with the youngsters and to loss of objectivity. When the youngsters were being unconsciously mirrored, staff too might find feelings aroused within them, such as jealousy of each other or paranoid suspicion perhaps that they were not sufficiently valued. Sometimes the intensity of their work relationships created tension within their family. Sometimes staff felt that the director and the organisation responded to their stress with inadequate care. Their need to feel cared for at times put the director under a similar kind of pressure to the pressure which the youngsters exerted on the staff themselves.

The director's style of leadership had disadvantages, despite its major advantage which helped to contain this exceptional situation safely. The centrality of his position in the programme, in the daily Community Meeting for example, aroused many feelings in the residents and staff that they shared, especially those which concerned relationships with authority. The clarification of issues about authority should be an ongoing task in a group of adolescents, but when the director's resilience was reduced by unusual demands for his attention or by outside issues perhaps, his response could be defensive in a way that prevented the resolution of conflict.

The director was constantly aware that the youngsters' actual lives, and certainly their futures, were often at real risk and that although it was necessary to accept disturbed behaviour as a step on the road to normal functioning, it was equally therapeutically essential to ensure stability. The Community may have appeared to be without rules, but maintaining a relaxed appearance required that the carefully developed underlying structure was adhered to meticulously.

Sometimes staff felt that the director's seemingly obsessive and restrictive insistence on this hampered their growth and creativity. It may well be that, in fact as well as fantasy, the staff could have been managed with greater sensitivity. Different styles of leadership have different advantages, of course. However, if overcoming obstructions to the Community's development and keeping everyone focused on the real task of the organisation was essential, it certainly was what particularly derived from this style. It could also be argued that a different style is needed as a community matures (Rose 1990), but the capacity to maintain an adolescent community's focus and motivation remains essential to its survival. The director felt that he was pragmatic and he made no apologies for his singlemindedness whenever he felt that the paramountcy of the youngsters' needs should be emphasised. This focus created stability and security, but it also created conflict even if the balance between the youngsters' needs and the staff's was usually maintained.

ARTHUR Towards the time that I left, I was subtly made aware that there were some significant differences of opinion between N. and M.

The significance of these differences is debatable. N. was one of the two visiting consultant psychiatrists with whom the director had worked for sixteen years. That itself indicates how much was actually shared in terms of approach and professional ideology. Her contribution to the fundamental therapeutic structure and to the effective therapeutic style of Peper

Harow was one of its most important elements. However, in such an emotionally charged environment, differences are hard for everyone to manage.

It is difficult to imagine how a group of people could engage without disagreement in such a complex enterprise, one that made such demands on everyone's personality. At the same time, whenever and for whatever reason anxiety was raised, commitment and growth were inhibited.

Another professional hazard in a therapeutic environment is the way that the normal range of human immaturity, including conflict, tends to become interpreted in a quasi-psychoanalytic fashion (Baron 1987). Proponents of one interpretation would argue that their objective was to clarify, though they may well have been less conscious of their underlying wish to justify their own side of an argument. Although attempts were constantly made to manage these problems, they were never overcome instantly. All staff received regular and frequent casework supervision and support. A combined system of outside organisational consultants and senior staff was developed, in order to help staff to reflect on their individual work and on their work in groups, and as part of the organisation as a whole. Its different elements took up nearly a third of each member of staff's working hours. Sometimes it seemed as though there could never be enough time for reflection and an arbitrary line had to be drawn. However, the system did take several years to become maximally effective, so that Spencer's speculation could well have been a reasonable concern at one stage in the Community's development.

SPENCER I realise that the staff did get counselling whilst they were working there, but I do wonder if they got the right kind of supervision.

Until the system of supervision was fully developed, there were inevitably problems that inhibited the therapeutic process. One serious problem mentioned by several ex-residents, concerned an accusation of sexual abuse by a member of staff. Though he denied the accusation, the problem was not entirely well managed. Had the supervision system been fully developed at the time of the alleged incident, it might have prevented whatever did happen – if it did. Some ex-residents are sure that the accusation was accurate, while others disagree. Although the incident was taken very seriously at the time and the accused adult left the Community, the complexity of abuse in institutions had not been openly and professionally explored in the early 1970s. Although the actual organisational response turned out to be very similar to that currently recommended by government guidelines, the incident was not resolved clinically as well as it could have been. Insufficiently prepared, everyone was taken aback by their complex reactions. Staff were caught between hoping the accusation was untrue, while still wanting to respond appropriately. During the last twenty-five years we have learned that the initial reaction to such issues usually tends to be confused. Therefore, a previously thought-through procedure has to be structured into the organisation in anticipation. It should be designed to ensure that incidents are fully resolved and also that residents and staff both feel fully supported. At the time, despite the attempt to discuss the incident in the Community Meeting, the staff were not clear how they felt and so it is not surprising that their uncomfortable response was misunderstood. Some youngsters inevitably experienced the incident as a betrayal, not just by the accused individual, but by the director and staff as a group.

> BERNIE That was the biggest level of let-down by M. His principle of putting us first was compromised at that point. He should've known that what we were thinking and feeling was the truth.

The youngsters assumed that the staff did not believe them, or that the staff's integrity could not be trusted, and this at a moment when the confused and frightened youngsters especially needed support. Staff felt both guilty and rejected and the impasse undermined the basic principle of a therapeutic relationship. Experience teaches that there are definitely situations when it is better to share inadequacy and failure with adolescents than to pretend to a transparently unrealistic competence. It is even better to have a structure in place that helps staff to manage appropriately when they feel personally overwhelmed.

Today, residential institutions are required to report such accusations to their local authority's child protection unit immediately. Obviously, this enables independent professionals to examine the issue objectively. Although an established system such as this can at least address the primary issue of the allegations themselves, it may also produce other problems. Such situations sometimes traumatise the youngsters and adults still further. As in a family, it is best if the adults and the youngsters together are enabled to work through what has happened, so that neither are rendered helpless and with their positive identity undermined. The potential of injurious conflict may exist within any child protection issue, as has been seen both in Orkney and in Cleveland (Clyde 1992; Butler-Sloss 1988). It may seem that, on the one hand, the organisation, or the family members, can be injured by the well-intended protection procedures or, on the other hand, injured children can be left in an especially vulnerable situation (Kilpatrick 1992). These alternatives are not, of course, inevitable. Provided that such eventualities have been thoroughly prepared for in advance, conflicts of interest can at least be managed, if not entirely avoided (Schimmer 1993). This preparation should apply equally to the whole issue of sexuality and its management in the residential setting. It is discussed further in Chapter 6, Benefit of Hindsight.

Another problem that might have been managed better had we known in advance what has since been learned from these issues, related to the therapeutic development of the environment. Peper Harow as an Approved School had been decorated and furnished in what would have been regarded as an adequate though somewhat spartan style. With the dismantling of the Approved School's system of disciplined cleaning and maintenance, together with the abolition of corporal and all other forms of punishment and before an alternative system had been developed, the material condition of the environment had deteriorated. Life felt less straitjacketed, but it also became physically squalid. In the empty 20 foot high corridors and state rooms, every adolescent shriek and broken window echoed in a permanently disruptive racket. An alternative seemed to be the possibility of designing the daily material experience so that it would promote similar good feelings to those a baby enjoys and which many youngsters at Peper Harow had not. The form of that experience had to be suitable for adolescents, of course.

Thus the Community became furnished and decorated in a style that was in contrast with its wild beginnings. The general environment began to quieten and in some ways produced a greater sense of security. However, although youngsters who joined the Community at this time, or after the refurbishment had occurred, appreciated the quality of the environment, as Max, Sam and Solly inform us (Chapter 4, pp. 78, 82), many of those who had been in the Community since its beginning were not happy at the change.

> WILF Until the middle of '74, I and a lot of my friends could relate to the roughness of the place. It was a very big building. It wasn't furnished softly. It was pretty cold in places, but there were a few of us who always made sure there was wood and always fires. We had that sense of community. We had gatherings where we'd get together and sing and play music. Then about a year before I left, M. started investing into soft furnishings. A lot of us felt very constrained by it. You were told that the reason you couldn't accept this stuff was that you didn't feel good enough about yourself and that is rubbish.

The pain for some youngsters of acknowledging that Peper Harow was offering the kind of nurture that had not been lovingly provided by their erstwhile mother seemed unbearable at times. However, denying reality was, as ever, self-defeating. Attacks on psychotherapy, or on the therapist, seem to emphasise the very issue that Wilf, in this instance, is trying to deny.

Yet even if the problem of resistance to whatever symbolised emotional nurture explains some people's hostility to the physical changes, Wilf's comments also reveal another important issue. The Community was effective above all, because within its environment the residents knew that they really were the most important element of the whole enterprise and the adolescent lifestyle in which they lived confirmed this. The beginning of their individual sense of worth arose because they were sure of the pre-eminence of the residents' group and they were sure of their membership of that group. The material change within the house that Wilf refers to made for a considerable modification of their lifestyle. Even if that change was a necessary therapeutic progression, because it compelled the residents' group to function in a more adult fashion, the implied question that Wilf's criticism poses is whether the transition could have been accomplished with greater recognition of the significance of youngsters' sense of their ownership of the Community. Perhaps the loss of this sense of ownership of the group's lifestyle aroused their deeper and diffused sense of unmourned loss, especially for those with the least maternally caring backgrounds. Indeed, the very attention given to the maternally symbolising aspects of the physical environment, and especially within the house itself, perhaps made youngsters anxious that their new sense of personal worth and significance may have been illusory after all.

The material development of the Community represented a major organisational transition. The youngsters' response seemed similar to what had occurred when the initial change from an Approved School to a therapeutic Community had taken place. This also seems true of another major transition that occurred when girls joined the Community. By then it was clear how disruptive major changes to a community's lifestyle always are and how easily threatened is its apparently well-established sense of identity. However, at the time it was assumed that, even if some initial disruption was inevitable, after approximately three years the youngsters would have come to terms with the new situation and the Community would have begun to function effectively once more. It was not clear, however, how much more difficult the boys would find it to help very disturbed girls to become an integrated part of the residents' group as a whole. Once more there was an upsurge in the kind of behaviour that had been a major reason for the referral of both boys and girls (Table 2, Chapter 3, p. 59). The girls bullied each other in ways that had not been seen in Peper Harow for some time. Many youngsters left too soon for their own good, because of their feelings about the disruption. Yet, even those who arrived from approximately 1980 onwards and who had no personal experience of a more stable period, are still clear that Peper Harow had a major influence on the way they have lived since, even if it has taken much longer for them to recognise that value.

> SHARON Peper Harow is the most precious thing in my life. Without it, there would have been no hope for me.

And this from someone whose violence was such that she was eventually asked to leave!

The criticisms expressed earlier in this chapter by Spencer, Arthur and Wilf, for instance, about the management of staff and of the environment, correctly suggest that the interrelated clinical or organisational issues were not always well handled. Yet irrespective of managerial judgement, some of their criticisms may also have arisen from their failure to recognise the extent of psychopathology in the youngsters' group as the result of early emotional deprivation. There was certainly pathological resistance to insight by ex-residents when they were adolescents, and some misunderstanding of the therapeutic objectives may still remain.

However, while the ex-residents' negative comments help to reveal some of the unsolved problems that existed at Peper Harow, they do not express the opinion of all the ex-residents. Hamish's view of the material transformation of the environment is different from Wilf's, for example.

> HAMISH On Saturday morning we used to do a huge clean-out of the whole house. I used to love working in the dining room, vacuuming, polishing gorgeous oak tables. Kids who arrived after me wouldn't have the experience of living in a draughty house and seeing it grow. Seeing your own growth being rewarded. You did think, 'I can feel myself progressing a bit. I deserve this comfortable settee.'

Control and treatment are exceptionally interdependent in such an institution. The balance is a fine one, for behaviour needs to be examined with as few value judgements as possible if it is to be used as a key to an individual's unconscious functioning. Yet, as Sharon's experience shows, if behaviour cannot be controlled – which begs a series of questions about the methods by which control is obtained – the consequences may be too disruptive to be tolerable.

Nevertheless, this chapter focuses particularly on that early damage to many residents' personalities that makes them resistant to change, even when their attitudes and behaviour have been fundamentally altered and even in the face of their new-found ability to manage successfully. In several cases, a deep uncertainty can still be detected about whether they feel they deserve their success and about whether it is real or secure. Occasionally, self-doubt rises to the surface, generating impulses which, if acted upon, would confirm their negative image rather than strengthen their hard-won achievements.

Becoming a parent, one of life's ultimate moments of joy, is just the kind of pleasure to be adulterated by such an echo of the ex-resident's own very different infancy. How hard it is to avoid envy. The slightest stirring of negative feeling and anxiety threatens once more. Perhaps Harold's denial that his own infancy and childhood were especially painful is an example of the reassertion of his old unconscious defences in the face of that threat.

> HAROLD My mum and dad split up when I was about one year old. My mum is gay, but I don't know if that was a factor at the time. They both suffered physically. My dad had blackouts . . . My mum was fairly drug dependent. This is all stuff that I found out later. They split up and my sister and I spent a year at a children's home . . . I spent a year in a children's home when I was about six or seven. I think that my mum was in and out of hospital . . . As far as I was concerned at the time, everything was tickety-boo.

It seems extraordinary that Harold's current reaction to this series of major family problems is that 'everything was tickety-boo'! Several ex-residents felt that they had no alternative to putting on a brave face in response to the frequent, painful experiences of their childhood. Of course, many people's unexpected traumatic experiences do require a level of resilience and staunch forbearance and, if they had been fortunate, their earlier lives would have developed such strengths. Though life may be painful, most adults have the psychological ability to cope amazingly. However, when youngsters at Peper Harow denied that anything had been particularly wrong in their early lives, they were not exemplifying their mature emotional strength. Instead, their denial of reality illustrated that their past was still too painful to acknowledge, irrespective of the therapeutic imperative.

Hamish, though, claims that having learned at Peper Harow to avoid denying uncomfortable feelings, he has fundamentally changed his ability to manage, rather than to deny, stress within his current life.

> HAMISH Peper Harow is very much part of our marriage. We have the normal amount of arguments and sometimes one of us has done something that the other doesn't like . . . Peper Harow taught me to talk through my feelings, instead of carrying on being unhappy and then saying, 'I've had enough' and going.

Hamish's ability to cope with his family and career is impressive. In comparison with his life before Peper Harow, his achievement contrasts even more remarkably. And yet even so, within his transcript can still be found the occasional comment whose tone seems to contradict those achievements. For example, he describes situations when he has nearly been caught out, in a way that still frightens him, by an unexpected re-emergence of his adolescent depression and other personality problems.

> HAMISH I had to move from my last job because I felt that people didn't appreciate what I was trying to do. Sometimes I do have a problem with self-esteem, which is something I have always had. I do still get occasional bouts of depression. I can't say if these are normal depressions, or if they are special to me because of my background.

Hamish's real achievement is to be aware of the problem. From his therapeutic experience at Peper Harow, he has also learned how to manage its consequences. If his personality had not matured, he would still be too apprehensive to allow himself to identify such feelings as depression. And yet despite that, an inappropriately gleeful quality occasionally colours his reminiscence of some of his very seriously anti-social adolescent behaviour.

> HAMISH There are certain things that I no longer remember. Apparently I nearly derailed an express train . . . Apparently I'd put some sleepers on the line. They were removed before the train came by. It's a bit exciting to think about what might have happened.

Are Hamish's inconsistent memory and use of the word 'exciting' perhaps a form of defensiveness against his burden of shame, or does he still preserve some minimal fear for his sanity?

> HAMISH My mother had told me that my father was a psychopath. When things started to go wrong at home, I came up with the very juvenile idea that I was a psychopath also. I had inherited it from my father.

While any traces of Hamish's past problems are as nothing compared with his achievements, they do raise the question of how seriously we should regard ex-residents' denial of current difficulties. Do examples of such denial simply demonstrate normal psychosocial functioning, which are therefore bound to include inevitable limitations of insight and not just psychological strengths? Or do those examples reveal that, however much has been resolved their lives continue to be affected by outstanding problems which they compulsively try to conceal?

HENRY I still get quite drunk now and again, but it's not really a problem.

This may be true for a young adult in the weekly environment of his local rugby club, but those who know Henry in his late thirties might feel that it would be more accurate to say that heavy drinking indicates at least a kind of emotional discomfort, even if it is one that he feels is manageable.

It is difficult to believe that what Albert says of himself does not constitute a problem. From the rest of his transcript it is easy to believe that the kind of person he aspires to being would not behave as he describes, even rarely.

ALBERT I'm not a violent person . . . I do feel guilty when I find myself smacking the children . . . from an argument I had with Val . . . I hit her a couple of times, but not much. They threw me in a cell and put me in court the next morning.

It is as though the malign emotional circumstances that originally set such aggression in train, still preserve some hold on the predominantly altered adult. When Bernie, for example, describes the material poverty of his childhood, or when Lenny speaks of his mother's rejection, it is easy to understand how such injuries might well take a lifetime to overcome.

Yet some ex-residents seem to find difficulty in acknowledging how painful life was before Peper Harow. They say little that fully reflects the misery, terror and anguish of their childhood experiences.

EDMUND I tell Judy about how my mum used to hit me with a horse-whip. Judy says, 'That's really bad!' but at the time when you are there, it's just normal.

Edmund speculates about other parents' loss of temper with their children, as well as his, and then he concludes that it was the unpredictability about the way that his father used to beat him that caused him to withdraw emotionally. The pervasive insecurity that arises from unpredictable trauma is especially hard to overcome. Fear and pain so generated seems to have no boundaries, which makes it very difficult later in life to exchange compulsively defensive reactions for warmth and spontaneity.

By seeking help, Bruce's parents may have conscientiously recognised the need to avoid just such a re-enactment of their own problems in their relationships with him.

BRUCE My parents took me to a child psychiatrist. They were a bit freaked out that things weren't going the way they wanted them to go, so they went looking for some help. I was labelled as depressed and troublesome. I was willing to accept whatever they said.

Although Bruce seems to imply that he accepted this diagnosis simply in order to make things easier for his parents, it seems unlikely that he went as far as becoming an in-patient in a mental hospital simply to placate them. If the implications of his comments are that the real family problem lay with his parents' difficulties and that his problems were simply a reflection of that, he may well be right. Nevertheless, his violent reaction while in hospital and his determined resistance to adults when he first came to Peper Harow reminds one that, irrespective of their original source, Bruce's serious problems had become his own by that time.

Eric finds it difficult to recall any endless sequence of violence or deprivation. As a consequence he feels he has even less justification for his inappropriate behaviour.

> ERIC   I always felt a bit of a fraud, because there were some kids there who had had a bloody awful life before they got there. In comparison, I've had it bloody easy.

Obviously, those who referred Eric to Peper Harow did not consider him to be a fraud in terms of his needs and they were mightily concerned about his behaviour. The defensiveness which underlies such a comment is not conscious. Nor is the comment only defensive. It also demonstrates Eric's compassion for others and perhaps some of his anxious feelings about his siblings who were left at home, or about his assessment of his current worth, compared with his wife and his own children.

All the interviewees are certain that they were not happy prior to life at Peper Harow and also that their childhood behaviour was unacceptable, especially when seen from their current adult and parental perspective. Yet their acknowledgement still seems ambivalent, as though they do not really wish to acknowledge exactly how abnormal their behaviour was. This ambivalence seems to apply particularly to their willingness to acknowledge how much they had been hurt and how much they had been psychologically damaged, as well as how abnormal their behaviour was. Henry's lifelong uncertainty as to who his family actually are, may explain how vague he appears to be about who the targets of his hatred are.

> HENRY   I used to design weird and wonderful weapons, razors stuck on the end of broomsticks, for example. Walking around with these used to terrify the staff and sent people scurrying for cover.

The emphasis is on 'terrifying the staff' and the tone of his phrase 'scurrying for cover' is arguably jocular, whereas a different memory of these events reminds one that other insecure residents bore the brunt of fear, for it was they who were most likely to be injured by razor blades buried in soap and under the handrail of the stairs.

The apparent delinquent glee with which other ex-residents still seem to want to deny the seriousness of their past behaviour calls into question how stable they feel their present lives actually to be.

> GAVIN School was a hoot! I've been chucked out of four schools in total. The last one capped it all. The boy next to me needled me a bit, so I had a go at him. I was hitting him and he wasn't hitting me back, which is the kind of fight that I like. Someone grabbed me from behind. I picked up a heavy steel stool and hit them with it. It was the physics teacher! After that, no school would have me. So it was off to the assessment centre. I did a few bursts in the special unit and solitary confinement. Then I arrived at Peper Harow. I was pretty sane compared to some of the lads.

Why is it still so hard to give up the underlying flippant cockiness demonstrated by Gavin? Psychodynamically, one might understand inappropriate behaviour as having originated from a misconceived way of responding to negative experience. Perhaps one unconscious motive for their behaviour is in order to hurt the person who had hurt them, even if realistically that person could never or can no longer be specifically identified. It is as though they do not entirely want to abandon their secretive, sadistic feelings, as though without these they would be without weapons and vulnerable once more. Some ex-residents, like Lenny or Eric, who come from seemingly intact families, find it even harder to identify who had actually hurt them, or exactly what had been done to them. Perhaps their response, irrespective of its particular form, has become an habitualised one, though it is bound to remain as ineffective as it always was in terms of resolving painful experience for very long. Banging one's head against a brick wall always turns out to be an ineffective way of getting through to the other side.

The essential psychotherapeutic process of clarifying underlying painful experiences requires a context that is secure. Although the sense of security at Peper Harow generally allowed the therapeutic process of the everyday lifestyle and environment to operate, something more was required to help individuals such as Gavin or Henry to identify precisely what they were trying to express, or who they had originally been trying to hurt or punish. It might well take a very long time before they could feel safe enough to live without the potential secret weapon of their behaviour. Only then would they be motivated to give up such attitudes wholeheartedly.

There were aspects of the therapeutic process itself that did not make for a sense of security. Although 65 per cent of the research participants felt that the Community Meetings were generally helpful, examination shows that many youngsters also found them stressful. Even the generally appreciated relationship with the individual's guru was undermined by his or her uncertainty about trusting someone who might not be perfect. And this ambivalent attitude applied to relationships with the peer group as a whole. Never having fully learned how to tolerate the inevitable element of uncertainty in relationships, it seems as though it felt safer to resist trusting any relationship and to deny anyone's caring, rather than to face the pain of possibly being let down – once again!

> LENNY Relationships had always been a problem for me at Peper Harow . . . If you were just trying to help someone, that wasn't a problem. It was with really close relationships, where you had a real friend. I found it very hard to share anything. I found it very difficult to handle rejection . . . I was always thinking that I was going to be rejected.

Nothing can absorb adolescents more than their affairs of the heart, even though their experimental love affairs may throw them from euphoria to despair. However, what can the psychosocial rough and tumble of those normal adolescent experiments be like for the youngster whose tentative explorations in the borderlands of adulthood do not spring from the security of early maternal love, or whose maternal care had been inconsistent and unreliable? The response in many of the transcripts reveals the ex-residents' wariness towards commitment within relationships at Peper Harow. It is hardly surprising that inconsistent primary relationships in infancy and childhood would make later loving relationships both desired yet immediately inhibited by the fear of rejection. By the time of adolescence, the individual may have decided that anyone's contact with them was doomed to failure and, moreover, that something within themselves was to blame.

> SHARON Then I went to a place . . . called Badger Vale. A week after I was there, they decided to shut it down. I thought it was because I was so naughty.

Wilf tries to put the sense of his ultimate worthlessness in the past but his ambivalence insists on making itself felt.

> WILF A lot of us felt that we were nothing more than shit, prior to Peper Harow. That will probably be there for the rest of my life.

Bettelheim explores similarly profound and pervasive damage to an individual's sense of self-worth in his essay, *Children of the Holocaust*

(Bettelheim 1990). The circumstances of those children's traumatisation may have been different though not the result. He asks:

> Why were the young victims unable to speak about what happened to them? Why is it even some twenty or thirty years later, so very difficult for them to talk about what happened to them during their childhood?
>
> (*ibid.*: 217)

Bettelheim quotes one survivor's comments.

> For years, my misery lay in an iron box buried so deep inside me that I was never sure just what it was. I knew it carried things more secret than sex and more dangerous than any shadow or ghost. Ghosts have a shape and name. What lay inside my iron box had none. Whatever lived inside me was so potent that words crumbled before they could describe it . . .
>
> Things thus repressed so deeply nevertheless seem to have an independent existence that corrodes one's life, destroys the right to enjoy things, even the feeling that one has a right to live.
>
> (*ibid.*: 218)

In addition he demonstrates that even when the 'Children of the Holocaust' grew up to live apparently normal lives, they still passed on to their own children, through some unconscious process, their own sense of emptiness, of unworthiness to live, their sense of alienation.

Even when there appears to be no evidence of early emotional deprivation, let alone physical abuse and traumatisation, the sense of alienation described by Harold, Ralph and others seems to be similar. Lenny's father's regular physical absence from home may well have symbolised his emotional absence, or alienation, even when he was physically present. He certainly had endured appalling traumatic experiences as an adolescent during the Second World War. Perhaps, therefore, what he had found too terrible to talk about had also been unconsciously passed on to Lenny. Others, like Rupert, report traumatic incidents in their early childhood that could not of themselves have occurred had there not been some pre-existing dysfunction in their family relationships from their earliest infancy. Perhaps Rupert's inability to put that experience into words is what still causes his current sleep problems.

RUPERT I still have terrible trouble sleeping on my own. I get really nervous and frightened. I had terrible nightmares as a kid.

Bettelheim's essay

> centred on the lack of mourning rather than on the horrors suffered by those we learn about . . . I have concentrated on the mourning because . . . in mourning one speaks about what one has lost and in doing so one talks mainly to oneself, but in front of a person who is ready to carry part of this burden, who understands, wishes to help. It is this which gives one the courage, the strength, to grieve, to be in a state of mourning.

> (*ibid.*: 229)

The specific loss that needed to be mourned if real healing of such wounds was to begin was different for each of those at Peper Harow, but the way in which they each still remained haunted was similar. It is as though the essence of what they each had lost was their childhood's organic and nurturing emotionality – as though they had been so paralysed by trauma and deprivation that emotion had lost its meaning. Not all our residents had experienced the extremity of abuse, but, as Lenny says:

> LENNY If someone loses their mother and someone loses their favourite pet, it's the same grief.

The purpose of his remark was to show that from the viewpoint of a child it is difficult to compare emotional pain and difficult to measure suffering. One way in which adults attempt to control the pain of loss is by categorising it on an artificial scale. Without an adult's repertoire of responses to emotional hurt, a child remains more vulnerable to long-term injury.

Clare Winnicott describes emotionally disturbed children as those who have lost contact with their past. Disturbed children need to 'mourn' their loss in some way, if they are ever fully to recover their full emotional capacity. She reminds us that

> small children, and even older ones, separated from their mothers, so often lose the capacity for speech, or lose the sense of the meaning behind the words . . . The words will no longer be a vehicle for communication and moreover, previous good experiences and the stored memories of them, which represent the inner world and true self, will remain cut off from present feelings and everyday life and growth will be impoverished or distorted.

> (Winnicott 1968: 66–67)

Mrs Winnicott reminds us that

All children who come our way have been through painful experiences

106

of one kind or another and this had led many of them to clamp down on feelings and others of them to feel angry and hostile, because this is more tolerable than to feel loss and isolation. To feel a sense of loss implies that something of value, something loved, is lost, otherwise there would be no loss. Awareness of loss therefore, restores the values of that which is lost and can lead in time to a reinstatement of the lost person and loving feelings in the inner life of the child. When this happens, real memories, as opposed to fantasies, of good past experiences can come flooding back and can be used to counteract the disappointments and frustrations which are also part of the lost past. In this way the past can become meaningful again. So many of the children we meet have no sense of the past and therefore they have no sense of the present and of the future.

(*ibid.*: 69)

The adolescents at Peper Harow usually did have a sense of the past, even if it was incomplete. Contact with it aroused their anxiety, for it too felt like 'the nameless shapeless horror in an iron box' (Bettelheim 1990). Their response to anxiety would be resistance and the eruption of defiant and destructive behaviours that took everyone's entire energies to subdue, and which simultaneously avoided any enquiry that might have given definable shape to that internal horror. Only confronting that insubstantial fear could confirm that those spectres were unreal. Yet how could the courage to confront be acquired when the therapeutic endeavour itself would inevitably trigger that very anxiety ?

At Peper Harow we certainly recognised the fear that underpinned these defences. No matter how aggressively they bullied others, they were still afraid themselves. Circumventing the youngsters' fear depended greatly on the quality of the individual relationships with staff whose worth was generally appreciated by the youngsters.

> HAROLD All the staff that were there when I first got there, were very authoritative. It felt very safe. They were very clear about who they were and what they were doing.

One might imagine that highly educated and competent adults might seem too culturally different from the youngsters for a real relationship to develop. But staff did not pretend to false authority. They could share the crazy adolescent lifestyle without standing on the dignity of their professional status, for instance. At the same time they had the capacity to listen with genuine compassion. This ability to listen sensitively was a fertile stimulus towards 'mourning the lost past' (Bettelheim 1990) and melting the ice in their psyche.

When the group as a whole was at its most self-confident it had an exceptional capacity for sharing the individual's burden. Nevertheless, the gurus' reaction might feel more predictable than the peer group's, which is perhaps why several ex-residents seem to have valued their guru more than the groups.

> BERNIE I don't think my Peper Harow experience did me a lot of good in terms of group work. I can't remember saying anything profound, or getting in touch with my emotions. It was pretty much the same as the Large Group. I spent most of my time fending off feelings.

Despite this, Bernie could still offer profound insights in all group settings, both about himself and about the Community as a whole. Once, in the face of the delinquent and manic tomfoolery that had been the Community's entrenched response to the current problem of food stealing, Bernie spoke of the deprivation that he and many others had experienced as children. His comments triggered a dramatic change of mood that stimulated several other youngsters to speak movingly of the time when they had actually begun to steal from their mothers. I make no claims that my memory is more accurate than Bernie's, only that memory reflects as much about one's ongoing internal life as it does about the facts it attempts to communicate. Bernie is acutely conscious of his feelings of alienation. Others remember his humanity.

Mrs Winnicott's paper 'Communicating With Children' (Winnicott 1968) demonstrates clearly that our initial motivation to learn to speak is derived at least partly from our need to symbolise mother. The significance of words is unconsciously rooted in our earlier emotional experience and is stimulated or inhibited accordingly. When Bernie says that he 'spent three years waffling . . . and no one was aware of that', he may be forgetting that he probably needed to waffle, in the same way that a baby needs to babble, as part of the process of mastering the meaning in words. What was difficult for Bernie and for staff to understand with sufficient confidence, is that 'waffling' may not only denote a withholding of meaning and a refusal to respond with emotional warmth to the Community's caring attention. His apparently empty words may also symbolise the lengthy struggle needed before anyone could become sure of his or her desire to communicate and to promote the development of meaningful language. Bernie certainly reminds us that no therapist has a magic key to 'the iron box' any more than has the suffering individual within whom the box is buried. When the 'meaning behind the words' (Winnicott 1968: 66–67) has been lost, or never fully established, it may take much longer to find that meaning than it normally takes to learn to speak. Recovering the relationship between language and emotionality depends as much on the capacity of the therapist to remain persistently close to the patient for a very long time as it does on the courage and persistence of the patient him- or herself. We also felt that the groups as well had a central role in this recovery. Perhaps their very threat confirmed their therapeutic significance, or there would have been less vehement resistance.

Some 82 per cent of the sample are enthusiastic about camps and expeditions. Even if they were aware that their purpose was also therapeutic, its threat was less direct.

> 'DUKE' I went on a couple of expeditions and they were good times. They were landmarks. Carrying loads of stuff across miles and miles of the Pennine Way. They were good times . . .
>
> It's old-fashioned to say that they were character-building, but they really were. I grew up a lot. You had to learn to look after yourself! You had to go out to the middle of nowhere, stick a tent up in freezing cold weather, cook your food. Having to do all that stuff was really good! Give me more of it! There was more therapy there than in a hundred Community Meetings. That was a growing time.

The technology of therapy hardly mattered to the youngsters. Their enthusiasm for studying and for expressing emotion, when their ability to do so had been set free, their sense of growth on mountains, in the art studios and when playing in the grounds – all these provided a major part of the psychotherapeutic process. However, the psychotherapeutic manifestation and working through of the individual's ghosts or 'acting out' behaviour and enduring the youngster's consequent depression was equally necessary. It may be that there is a limit to how much hurt or hurting behaviour can be coped with by either the adults on the receiving end or even the youngster him or herself.

Perhaps further therapeutic activity has to wait for later developmental opportunities in adulthood. What was essential at Peper Harow was whether their general functioning had changed sufficiently for growth to continue – and the overwhelming evidence of the ex-residents is positive.

The transcripts also remind us how complex it is to ensure that sufficient resources of any kind are skilfully enough managed to enable fundamental changes of attitude and direction, while at the same time ensuring that any factors that would undermine those changes are contained. When the enterprise to change Peper Harow from a training to a therapeutic establishment began, we were under no illusions that this would be anything other than difficult, or that we could grow without mistakes. The results nevertheless, would suggest that it was worthwhile.

6

BENEFIT OF HINDSIGHT

The ex-residents' criticism seems to be of two kinds. The first arises from their unfinished psychological business, which reveals itself in current relationship problems or perhaps in discordant social behaviour like heavy drinking. Unresolved psychological issues continue to make it difficult for some ex-residents to acknowledge how painful their childhood actually was, or how appalling their adolescent behaviour had been. Consequently, they still attempt to defend themselves against the extreme anxiety that some aspects of Peper Harow aroused in them by making disparaging comments about the material environment, for instance, or about individual members of staff. At the same time, many of their criticisms are accurate. The way the general growth and development of the Community was effected and the way its material environment was changed, and even comments about the quality of the professional supervision of staff, are all examples of this. Unfortunately, no organisation, especially one pursuing such complex objectives, can get everything right from the start. With the benefit of hindsight, perhaps some of those mistakes could be avoided today, which makes them well worth discussing.

Inevitably, the practical and the psychodynamic are interwoven. At the same time as we were trying to put an absolute embargo on inappropriate behaviour such as drug-taking or bullying or sexually abusive behaviour, our greater concern was to understand what the youngster's behaviour told us about his or her unconscious life, including what motivated inappropriate behaviour. To engage the youngster in an effective psychotherapeutic enquiry, value judgements needed to be suspended. However, although making sense of the youngster's behaviour offered real benefit in the long run, unacceptable behaviour often had to be controlled meanwhile, if the enterprise was to survive. Some respite from a normal social response to this behaviour was an essential privilege for the residents. Even so, there were limits to what was acceptable. Breaking the law, for

instance, went beyond them. Moreover, no one could be helped psychotherapeutically if everyone's attention was continually focused on the
latest behavioural crisis, such as who had run away or who had smoked a
'joint' in their bedroom. If talking about the painful past demanded great
courage for a fourteen-year-old, it became impossible if they were silenced
by a sneering bully. Without control of behaviour, there could be no
therapy and, ultimately, no Community at all.

And yet no one's behaviour, especially when they first came, could be
normal. Had they not been exceptionally destructive towards themselves
or towards others, in a variety of forms, no one would have referred
them. Until they had been at the Community for some time and had
begun to feel that they really did belong to the group, even their motivation to behave more acceptably was minimal. It was impossible to know in
advance who would succeed and who would leave within a few months.
Some of the most successful ex-residents wore staff's patience out with suicidal behaviour or with aggression and violence, for up to two years.
Some of them had been on the verge of exasperated expulsion many
times and yet, eventually, they were able to make the shift from negativity
to creativity and positive commitment.

> GAVIN Part of M.'s influence was the idea that you could do something
> for virtually anyone. M. wasn't pragmatic enough. He didn't say,
> 'Look you've been here a year, you're a waste of space. Off you go.' It
> was brutal, but then he could get in someone who might take advan-
> tage of the place. He couldn't do that because it would undermine all
> the confidence that was there.

Experience showed that, whenever anyone was on the verge of expulsion, everyone else's anxiety about whether they deserved to be there or
not was also aroused. Sometimes it seemed as if a queue had been formed
of hitherto appropriately functioning residents who were anxiously compelled to test out their entitlement yet again through suddenly enhanced
delinquent behaviour.

> LENNY Whenever anyone left [in inappropriate circumstances], I felt
> really awful. But I couldn't say it because other people would be
> saying, 'Driftwood. Forget about him. He was only here for a year and
> tried to set fire to the place twice. He's a bad 'un!' I thought, 'But this
> is Peper Harow! We're all bad 'uns!'

Gavin and Lenny represent opposite opinions of where the line of tolerance should be drawn. If one took too harsh a view, no one would
deserve to be there!

RUPERT The first couple of years were really difficult. I didn't know if I was going to make it. No one does . . .

Some people really needed confrontation. A lenient approach would have been disastrous for them. Rupert had been involved in hard drugs for some time before he came and there was a real doubt as to whether he should have been brought into the Community at all.

RUPERT M. thought that my drug problem was much worse than it really was . . . He said, 'You're going to do some crazy things while you're here.' He said that there would be times when I would feel bad and feel like giving it all up. 'That's normal. Don't give up!'

Fortunately, Rupert did not give up, though was a close run at times both at Peper Harow and in the first few years after he left. He still feels that he has outstanding problems, but he has done remarkably well despite them.

RUPERT You rely more or less on your comrades and peers. There were a few loners there, but it was very difficult to be alone in that place. You make friends, or you collude with people.
    There had been a group of us going off and taking drugs and there had been a lot of delinquent behaviour. That was the point that M. stepped in. There were nine people who had to say to the Community, 'We are going to be responsible. We are not going to take drugs.' This was a very significant incident.

It seemed essential that the possibility of compulsory closure by outside authorities should be recognised by the residents. Their commitment to a drug-free environment needed to be real, despite their own greater than average propensity to become involved in drugs. Extra Community Meetings were called for several days. Most of the collusive and delinquent 'gang of nine' were prepared to swear anything to avoid being thrown out – the old saying about an execution in the morning clarifying the mind – applies. However, one or two of them were overcome by almost suicidal compulsion to bring that very disaster about! For the Community as a whole, to get them to recognise that they could manage their panic and achieve a positive outcome instead required an extraordinary commitment by the peer group, and yet they did all rise to that occasion.

However, staff's anxious responsibility for adolescent behaviour is not improved by society's fantasies that offering treatment is being 'soft on young thugs'. Nor will defensiveness about issues like drugs or sex help to develop treatment programmes. Nor is it surprising that staff were hardly better able to distance themselves from the social attitudes of the times than most people. Social attitudes generally towards child abuse seemed almost conspiratorial. The change since then in the general attitude towards sexuality has been significant. Recognising how widespread the problem of sexual abuse of children actually is has forced the general public to acknowledge its seriousness. The more open societal attitude has enabled professionals to work harder to understand the potentially pathological consequences of sexual abuse. Research has made it increasingly possible to devise effective treatment programmes. No one claims that, despite the improvement, sexual issues do not still remain a difficult subject to explore in the face of so many contradictory societal attitudes. Nevertheless, the progress over the last twenty-five years is clear.

> BERNIE I can't remember any sexual activity while I was there . . . I was completely terrified of sex . . . Really, it was a blind spot for me. I don't see how Peper Harow could've done more work on this. They had no knowledge of sexual abuse. M. did acknowledge that lots of people in the Community had been abused. He was ahead of his time in that respect, but he still did not really know how to deal with it.

Research has shown how emotionally deprived and damaged children actually become especially vulnerable to being sexually abused, but also what its long-term effects are.

> GEORGIE I didn't have sex at Peper Harow. They were all so gross. I hadn't had sex before Peper Harow. I was sexually abused by my father, which made it quite hard. I find it quite hard still.

To have changed Georgie's remaining difficulties, we would have had to have understood more about the long-term consequences in order to have devised treatment that was more focused on the particular problems that arise from sexual abuse. 'Identification of the constellation of symptoms associated with traumatic abuse is essential if treatment is to be effective' (Zahn and Schug 1993: 68). Since that time, researchers of a special project for survivors of sexual abuse in the United States write that 'Severe symptoms have been observed in 46 per cent to 66 per cent of sexually abused children' (ibid.: 66).

> Sexually abused children have been found to exhibit a wide range of symptomatic behaviour and intrapsychic problems . . . symptoms that correspond to post-traumatic symptomatology can include enuresis, sleep disturbances, running away and truancy, learning problems, hyperactivity and inappropriate sexual behaviour. Intrapsychic problems

can include depression, anxiety and suicidal ideation . . . sexually abused children can also appear to have difficulty in interpersonal relationships . . . Several researchers have found links between sexual abuse and more serious problems such as psychosis and multiple personality.

According to traumagenic theory, survivors of traumatic sexual abuse may repeat or re-enact the abusive acts as a means of attempting mastery over the overwhelming conflict . . . traumatic memory remains active and unprocessed until such time as it can be therapeutically 'worked through' and placed into past memory. Behaviours that look 'perseverative' may actually be behaviours that are repetitions of the response to trauma, that have not yet been processed.

In residential treatment, re-enactment may also be observed in the acting out of power struggles with staff and peers and in eliciting negative and punitive responses from staff. Sexual abuse is an issue of 'power' and not only 'sexual desire'.

(*ibid.*: 68–70)

Bernie's transcript reveals how much he has come to understand in the last twenty years about his own sexual abuse. He refers particularly to the abuse of power in adults' relationships with children and to the issue of compulsive re-enactment by erstwhile abused children, but he also describes how much of his own inhibiting anxiety was due to the state of confusion in which his abusers had left him. He feels that if his abuse had been more clearly and specifically acknowledged, then at least the problems that had derived from his unresolved confusion as to where the responsibility for the abuse actually lay could have been avoided. His comments are illuminating and persuasive.

One is left to speculate whether the outcome of Sharon's appalling and violent behaviour, that eventuated in her being expelled later than the time of this study, could have been different had her initial psychotherapy at the Community focused on the issue of her prior sexual abuse. When Hamish, twenty years later says, 'I have a problem with low self-esteem . . . I do still get occasional bouts of depression', to what extent might that have been psychotherapeutically counter-balanced if the consequences of his sexual abuse had been directly addressed by a focused psychotherapeutic programme?

HERMIONE The sex issue was not addressed in a realistic way. If you had sex you were supposed to be thrown out, which was ridiculous . . . if it had been handled in a mature way, then maybe people would have progressed with it.

Today, the relationships between many kinds of trauma are underlined by the similarity of much of the symptology. Had this been understood then, perhaps effective programmes, such as those that have been developed for adults suffering from post-traumatic stress, for instance, might have pointed the way to programmes at Peper Harow specifically directed towards those suffering from the consequences of sexual abuse.

This is not to suggest that such programmes would have been adequate on their own. Indeed, because these programmes are so specific, it would have been important to ensure that energy still required for other psychotherapeutic and developmental needs was not diverted, leaving other issues unrecognised and unresourced. Most of our youngsters had not experienced only one major problem. Their sexual vulnerability had been caused in the first place by a series of deprivatory and traumatic experiences. Sex had attractions at Peper Harow beyond those experienced by normal adolescents. Many had been rendered desperate for attention, for any kind of physical contact, because of their severe emotional deprivation.

HERMIONE Basically, sex at Peper Harow was for comfort . . . To be more constructive, it should have been treated in confidence with certain members of staff. Helping people to understand what they were doing and to let them know that you can't just hide.

Serious deprivation not only causes behaviour that is dangerous to the youngster and to those he or she encounters, it also prevents their being able to use normal psychosocial experience as food for normal growth. The strength of Peper Harow lay in its attempt to respond to the whole person, rather than to a behaviourally categorised part. This study emphasises how effective that was generally. The improvement that hindsight offers is that special programmes for special kinds of injury were needed in addition.

However, if the management of sexual issues during the period of this study was not as successful as one would have wished, perhaps the consequences would have been worse had the rest of the programme not been successful. All the female ex-residents express their view that their experience was worthwhile, despite their criticisms of the management of sexuality. Nor was the limited management of sexuality gender-specific. Several comments in interview suggest that there had been homosexual liaisons among the boys even before the girls came and that those had been managed no better than any other sexual issue. Fifty-seven per cent specifically felt that sexuality in general was badly handled and another 14 per cent were unclear, but nobody felt that sexuality was well managed.

However, because the whole programme was geared to be sensitive and on the side of the youngsters, the staff's propensity, at least, was towards support rather than condemnation, even if we can now see that greater professional objectivity and skill were required. When Teresa describes the organisation as naive, later experience compels agreement.

> TERESA There was this big thing going on about not having exclusive relationships and you were fourteen, fifteen, sixteen and there were all those boys and you couldn't have a relationship with a boy. That was just ridiculous from the outset! To say, 'You shouldn't have sex', like they say, 'You shouldn't take drugs' . . . To say, 'You shouldn't be screwing under this roof', makes you want it even more. Of course they were going to have those problems at Peper Harow.

Experience taught that straightforward embargo would invariably be defied by adolescents and yet we naively assumed that, because trust had become well-rooted during the previous ten years, after some initial turmoil the staff's genuine concern for the youngsters' wellbeing would enable that mutual basic trust to reassert itself. A similar recovery of group responsibility had always occurred whenever issues that created conflict between adults and youngsters had been given enough time for the conflict to be resolved. The group continually had to reinforce its fundamental purpose – that of re-establishing a solid foundation for the rest of the residents' lives. It is difficult for adolescents to remain singleminded. Ideals founded on insecure personalities are even harder to keep on course. It is a tribute to the Community that, despite wanderings, it had always done so.

Nevertheless, both the views of adults and adolescents at the time were still too simple. What Hermione says about 'sex . . . was for comfort' is undoubtedly a real factor but, among such a disturbed population, it was still only one. The idea that time would allow the fundamentally healthy aspects of group functioning to reassert themselves fails to recognise that this could only happen if everything else – especially the staff – remained stable while this attitudinal balance was being re-established. It failed to acknowledge the destabilising effect of staff changes, for instance, that produced a compulsive upsurge of sexual behaviour, in addition to the usual upsurge of disturbed behaviour in response to any increase in anxiety.

Sexual activity of any sort among young residents presents many problems and few advantages from an administrative point of view. In addition to complex clinical and safety issues, staff members must also deal with the law.

(Schimmer 1993: 26–27)

Schimmer's comment highlights the contradictions which a residential establishment must somehow reconcile. Several of our youngsters had been involved in prostitution and promiscuous sex since they were pubescent. They needed time to learn to trust Peper Harow before they could begin to accept what was being offered, let alone begin to exert control over their sexual behaviour. They could hardly be expected to overcome their compulsivity between the day they arrived and the next, simply because they had changed their geographical location. Nor was time alone sufficient. An underlying objective of the environment was to create the nurturing experience that Gavin, like Henry, calls 'space'. But it was 'space' within which insight and awareness were also being stimulated. It did not just mean indulgence.

> GAVIN There was 'space' at Peper Harow. When I think back about what was important, I can see that 'space' was. If you were involved with something wrong, they would give you 'space'. If I wasn't in the mood, I probably wouldn't say anything. If I was, I did. You never think at the time, 'It's because he's giving me enough "space"', you think it's because you feel like it.

As Schimmer says:

> It is likely that the type of child so often seen in residence – a survivor of less-than-optimal early care, a member of an over-stressed, or fragmented family – may be one who is susceptible to engaging in sexual behaviour earlier and more frequently than the general population.
>
> Youngsters may join peer groups that rely heavily on sexual activity to compensate for affectionate nurturance that was unavailable in their families . . . the majority of their peers share similar histories and similar desires for restitutional intimacy.
>
> When it does occur, sexual behaviour may . . . involve the abuse or exploitation of residents, many of whom begin such activity as participants, but who emerge as traumatised victims.
>
> Residential treatment centres must protect residents and at the same time protect their healthy development. These may conflict unless staff members develop policies for the government of sexual behaviour of residents.

(Schimmer 1993: 23–27)

As with therapeutic programmes specifically focused on overcoming the consequences of sexual abuse, protection programmes can be designed within the context of an environment that still allows behaviour to express its unconscious roots in a psychotherapeutically spontaneous fashion. Nevertheless,

> Allegations of sexual abuse occur all too frequently in residential programmes. Their management is difficult because they elicit a great deal of anxiety, fear, guilt and feelings of vulnerability in the entire treatment and administrative systems. These feelings are compounded by concerns about accountability and liability which have escalated given recent mandated reporting and investigatory statutes.
>
> (Braga 1993: 81–82)

Chapter 5 suggests that protective intentions can sometimes turn out to have been harmful instead (pp. 95–96). Although developing policy that anticipates abuse is essential, many contradictory issues make this hard to do.

'Most young children need a lot more physical affection and admiration than they get . . . in children's homes' (Keith-Lucas 1993: 1–2), which again emphasises that we should take seriously what Hermione says about the need for comfort, even if we have to be sophisticated about managing its implementation.

> Since the discovery of the extent of child sexual abuse, even in children's homes, staff have had to be very careful. Almost any physical contact can be interpreted as abuse . . . Children . . . must be protected from unwelcome attention, but not at the cost of depriving them of one of their deepest needs.
>
> (*ibid.*: 2)

> Staff become quite angry . . . when confronted with evidence that their romanticised survivor is hurting other people. Their impression of the young person can change from that of an all good victim to an all bad offender. This is as dehumanising and non-therapeutic as treating the individual as a heroine.
>
> (Charles, Coleman and Matheson 1993: 15)

This change of attitude towards the youngster was also potentiated within the staff group by bullying and by other kinds of delinquent activity. Some youngsters begged to be scapegoated by staff and peers. It is, of course, unusual for suffering to enhance an individual's unselfish and caring instincts towards others. The opposite is much more likely to be true and yet, despite this, youngsters at Peper Harow were often told

No one understands the hurt of abuse more than you. No one, there-fore, should be able to help you more knowledgeably than you, yourselves. The 'contract' here amounts to just that, that you each try to care for each other, but that you definitely shouldn't add to each other's injuries and suffering.

It was never surprising that, despite the often moving interpersonal consideration which so many transcripts report, such an expectation inevitably proved somewhat unrealistic. Yet its existence did establish stan-dards of behaviour which most youngsters actually did achieve as they became more senior.

The law and social attitudes towards sexuality allow no room for the possibility of sexual abuse in residential establishments, which places its own constraints on helping the youngsters to repair the damaged roots of their psychosexuality.

On the other hand,

> safety and protection concerning sexuality is necessary in residential care, but not sufficient. Youngsters will attain *menarche*, will experience their first ejaculations and will have their first interpersonal sexual experiences while in group care . . . staff must accompany youth on their developmental journeys, uncomfortable though they may be . . . a style of government that balances safety and development [requires] continuous awareness of the nature and amount of sexual activity . . . being aware is of no use . . . if one does not understand it.
>
> (Schimmer 1993: 31–33)

Schimmer's article concludes with practical recommendations as to how a staff team might develop a policy that can reconcile these conflicting issues. Unfortunately, the advantages of such a policy in the 1970s and early 1980s were not clear to us. Many of the sexual issues were 'non-pathological, if highly problematic', as Schimmer puts it (*ibid.*). Much of the youngsters' sexual expression demonstrated their need for affection, their age-appropriate biological urges, the pressure on all adolescents by society as a whole for them to express sexuality. It is not abnormal that these earliest explorations of sexual intimacy would turn out to be exploitative, for this is a frequent stage on anybody's journey to adult sexual maturity.

However, many young people, while at Peper Harow, were not even able to cope with what would have been an appropriate level of problems for normal adolescence and especially with those problems that related to sexuality. Many had been sexually abused and so were too inhibited to make normal relationships, often feeling intensely jealous of others who did seem able to do so, and more uncertain about their own worth and sense of identity. Others compulsively acted out their past experiences promiscuously, feeling injured and undermined as a result. Yet others, who had been emotionally deprived in infancy, found powerful unresolved feelings of loss and hostility and of vulnerability aroused almost simultaneously with any spark of interest in the opposite sex.

Staff undoubtedly tried to support the young people through these problems, but were unclear about where the boundaries lay between what was normal and what was pathological. Where it was clear that help was needed, there was too little understanding of what would actually be helpful. If we had known then what the intervening two decades have forced us to recognise through the discovery of the extent of sexual abuse and its long-term effect on the abused, it is certain that the development of a precise policy and the methods of putting this into practice would have occurred. Staff development and training would not have simply created opportunities for staff to explore their own anxieties, but would have shed light on the relationship between the youngsters' psychosexual experience and their current behaviour. Training would have focused more specifically on what the staff's role and practice should have been.

It should be recognised that the complex and contradictory sexual issues that are inevitably faced within such a group, present managerial difficulties

> that may create an institutional ambivalence that permeates a sexual policy. Vacuous platitudes may displace substance and specificity . . . ambivalence may prevent the development of any sort of policy, reflecting serious confusion and a consequent ability to articulate a general agency position.
>
> (*ibid.*: 24)

A similar collapse into vacuous ineffectiveness may equally invade other aspects of a residential programme. There has always been concern about the poor level of education achieved by children brought up in children's homes, yet governmental bodies or their agents have been most resistant to understanding exactly why. It is easier for them to scapegoat staff generally for their supposed professional inadequacy than to define the complexities of educating young people whose psychological ability to learn and to form relationships was starved in their earlier life.

Despite the sensitive consideration which residents were able to give each other and the generally supportive environment of bedroom groups, which several transcripts emphasise, the ex-residents do not seem as enthusiastic about the helpfulness of peer-group relationships as one might have supposed. Only 59 per cent said that they were generally helpful and 35 per cent seemed either negative or unclear. Much of the fun they engaged in together, and many of the illicit sexual relationships, seemed to be as much to emphasise their independence from adults, whose values were at that moment being rejected.

As well as 53 per cent of the research participants feeling that sexuality was not well handled, 32 per cent also indicated that they were either bullied, or that they bullied others when they were at Peper Harow. This seemed to worsen after the admission of girls. Some people might feel that, compared with their previous experiences, the way bullying was addressed at Peper Harow was an improvement. However, the destruction of security that this caused and the inevitable undermining of the supposed values of the Community would make any bullying significantly damaging.

> VERA I'd have done better at Peper Harow if the girls hadn't been so bullying, if there'd been a better relationship between all the girls. If the whole thing had been sorted out earlier then maybe I might have got on better, but I was really fearful. If that had been dealt with then it might have worked. I never really settled in.

Peper Harow frequently came in for social workers' criticism for not trying hard enough to integrate the youngsters with their families, though overwhelmingly – 88 per cent of the sample of ex-residents – felt that Peper Harow's fairly arm's-length, albeit respectful, relationship with their family was appropriate. Nine per cent disagreed.

One reason for Spencer's brother being referred lay in the hope that some family re-integration could begin as a consequence.

> SPENCER I don't think that my relationship with my family changed at Peper Harow. We never grew up as a family and it has always been very fragmented . . . Obviously when Jonathan came to live at Peper Harow that affected our relationship. It was very difficult for me to accept his being there, for lots of reasons peculiar to me. I felt that he was a brat. I felt that he was going to take away something that I had and other things. It was very difficult to cope with. It was talked about and I feel that it was resolved eventually and when I left we became very close. It was a good thing that he went there and I'm glad. I regret that I couldn't sort things out more with him whilst I was there.

As well as Spencer's exceptional sibling rivalry, other features of family disturbance were reflected in the way youngsters functioned at Peper Harow.

SOLLY   I had this feeling that Peper Harow became almost like a family and you were playing one family off against the other.

The children of warring parents often feel pressured to take one parent's side or the other. Sometimes they enact their dilemma by attempting to polarise their parents and to identify one as the good parent and the other as the bad parent. Solly often tried to force Peper Harow into the symbolic role of one of these 'parent' figures. His guru was constantly having to· resolve situations that Solly had manipulated in order to set one 'parent' against the other. The resolution through awareness and consideration of what lay behind this compulsion to divide in order to control could not be described as family therapy, but it did address the issue of Solly's fractured family relationships. These were never entirely resolved. Solly has certainly developed ideas about what an integrated, rather than a fractured family would be like, from his actual experience at Peper Harow.

SOLLY   I think of that as my home, my family, the time when I grew up.

But positive though the overall group experience at Peper Harow may have been for Solly, it is still not the same as a well-functioning family. Nor could placement in a foster family have done any more to replace what Solly had not experienced.

Despite Henry's opinion, a substantial number of residents would not have agreed to come to Peper Harow if a condition had included their therapeutic involvement with their family.

HENRY   I think that this is an area where everybody is an expert in hindsight. I think that in reality a lot of kids would've benefited from counselling going on within their families in parallel with their own.

Only a minority thought that more should have been done about their relationships within their families. Bruce's tone suggests that he would have liked his relationships with his family to have been improved by Peper Harow and yet at the time he was also totally resistant.

BRUCE   My relationship with my family didn't change over the time that I was at Peper Harow. I think that they had a welcome break from it. I was being looked after better than I had been. They were happy that they didn't get the police on the doorstep in the middle of the night, or anything drastic. I seemed to be O.K. I was in the same place for a start. Because of the time and talking to gurus and in meetings there was a lot of talk about parents. That killed it for me. I think that the more I looked and the more I saw the less I wanted them. I wouldn't say that Peper Harow improved that relationship.

Maybe Peper Harow could've done more with my family, but I don't think that it would've been of any value to me. For me, it was enough to be dealing with my own problems. To be then dealing with my parents would've blown it. I was there for me. That's why my family weren't behind me. They didn't get any help and stayed the same. That's why they got divorced five years later.

Residents at Peper Harow were in the second half of adolescence and left at the time when they would normally be leaving home, especially if they had been successful educationally. Their desire to put some distance between themselves and their families had become an important and normal stage for them in the search for their own identity. Others, who had been in numerous children's and foster homes for their whole lives, had never developed any sense of family or home setting before Peper Harow. Many of the youngsters' families were more resistant to treatment than their children.

JERRY I went to Peper Harow to get away from my family. I remember going down to my house once with Edmund Tilman and he was trying to mediate between me and my mother and after a few minutes my mother had got him by the throat and was telling him her problems. I won't forget it and I don't think that Ed will. For most cases at Peper Harow, they needed to get them away from the families.

Jerry's view is shared by most ex-residents. When we consider Sharon's history (Chapter 3, pp. 33–35), it is difficult to see what would have been achieved had Peper Harow's policy been to develop a greater psychotherapeutic relationship with families. The complexity of some families' dysfunction could not possibly have been resolved in time for the youngsters to have been able to catch up with their own psychosocial and educational adolescent development.

SHARON I had no contact with my family whilst I was at Peper Harow. It was out of my control. I didn't want my dad to go to prison. He got two years for abusing me. I wanted him to get help. He needed to find out why he did what he did. It came to court before I went to Peper Harow. Peper Harow couldn't have done anything between me and my family. I was too confused for them even to understand *me*, let alone my family.

A major reason why many of these youngsters were finally placed at Peper Harow, as so many transcripts tell us, was because their family relationships had seemed to have become irreconcilable. Some have worked hard to re-establish a relationship with their families over the intervening years, but most positive family situations described in the transcripts are those with their own partners and offspring. We were certainly clear about the difference between family therapy and counselling. We were anxious not to pretend to offer family therapy, but we made a considerable effort to make families feel welcome rather than criticised. Our clear primary task was to change the direction in which the youngsters were travelling, before it was too late for them. We hoped that the nurture we offered would help them to become effective parents in time themselves, even if we felt unable to help change the whole family.

Nevertheless, a family flat was established to enable families as a whole to come and share a weekend's activities. Tea and cakes on a Sunday afternoon and dinner afterwards were always occasions when families were welcome. Gurus were expected to maintain a supportive relationship with families through regular communication. When parents visited they nearly always spent some time on their own, or together with their youngster, talking with staff specifically about family issues. Although youngsters were assured that the place being offered was for them personally, they were also told that it was hoped that they would be able to re-establish a better relationship with their family over time. We hoped we would be able to help family relationships not to deteriorate further. Of course, we were regularly reminded that the youngster could only be understood in the context of his or her family relationships, whether these had been positive or not. One of the conditions set at the initial interview was that during the youngster's first term, he or she and their guru should make a home visit together, sometimes extending overnight, in order to begin a personal relationship. In addition, the family would be invited to Peper Harow for a visit. After that, contact would depend on the youngster, though obviously great efforts to keep the contact going were made.

When we reflect on the difference demonstrated in Table 1 between those who had appropriate relationships within their families before they came to Peper Harow and those who demonstrate appropriate family relationships now, even if not with their parental families, we see a dramatic change. Nine per cent had positive relationships before Peper Harow and 68 per cent do so now, albeit more with their own families than with their parental family. Something about their capacity to maintain intimate relationships must have caused this change. At Peper Harow, amidst the quarrels and interpersonal exploitativeness and occasional expression of tenderness, their profound difficulties in relating to others appropriately were discussed as the issue of supreme importance on numerous occasions. This continuous emphasis undoubtedly had some effect. Many transcripts describe the influence of meetings at Peper Harow on the way the ex-residents tackle family problems today.

Whether they were adequately prepared for leaving is yet another issue that received significant criticism. Fifty-nine per cent are negative, while 29 per cent feel that they were adequately prepared. Within the files there is also some incomplete evidence about this. The file entries, of course, were predominantly contributed by staff. They suggest that 68 per cent were appropriately prepared although 22 per cent were not. This is a significantly different picture. How much the ex-residents' comments reflect their feeling that they were not ready to cope on their own, despite their determination to try, and how much do they reflect a straightforward and justifiable criticism of the inadequacies of the Peper Harow programme?

> BEN The leaving is the main criticism of Peper Harow. I suppose that it depends how prepared you are for it.
>
> I suppose that I had been there for four-and-a-half years and that was enough to really come to terms with what had happened and to understand what had gone wrong. It was also just long enough to have got out of the habit of doing things. But a lot of people went straight to higher education, having done 'A' levels at Peper Harow.

As Ben suggests in his transcript, he had not been able to be one of the 'high flyers' at Peper Harow. The question is how much had he actually received, despite his overt resistance. In fact, he has become outstandingly successful since, but he could not have foreseen this when it was decided that he was not going to make further progress within the Community.

> BEN The problem with help in leaving is that you don't actually realise that you need it until after you've gone . . . The leaving was almost as dramatic as when I first went there.

Many youngsters resisted help with leaving only to make the same discovery as Ben. However, sometimes their independent urge was justified.

> HENRY I decided a year before I left to see if I felt O.K. about actually leaving. I set myself a date for leaving in Summer 1979. I deliberately left with nowhere to go. I discussed this with Harry James [his guru]. It was my stubborn independent streak. A lot of people were going to university and things like that were set up, which felt O.K. for them. But I felt that the only true test of my independence was whether I could go out there and do it.

It is easy to under-estimate how stressful children from the most ideal families find leaving home as young adults. Knowing that they will always

have a loving family is an undoubted advantage for them, but their unconscious psychological competence to tolerate stress, while continuing to
address life positively, is an even greater advantage. Peper Harow could
never make up for the absence of an ideal family and we never claimed
that we could solve all the youngsters' problems. However, we did hope
that the residents would have changed enough by the time they left for
them to be able to cope on their own, even if they themselves felt unsure
of this at times. The results a generation later demonstrate that they were
able to cope, albeit with difficulty. Some are only just coming to recognise
their strength now.

Considering the level of psychosocial disturbance that residents at Peper
Harow had experienced before they arrived, it is amazing how much
they changed while they were there. The ex-residents who made up the
research sample are mostly in their thirties, and they have thought and
talked about their experiences at Peper Harow a great deal since they were
adolescents. Many have families of their own, in addition to experiencing
the difficulties of everyday life common to us all. Their current comments
about Peper Harow's worth are therefore founded both on their perception as normal adults and on their experience as adolescents with
exceptional difficulties.

They offer criticisms of every area considered in this study, even while
their overall enthusiasm remains remarkable. Frequently, ex-residents have
negative feelings at the same time as their predominantly enthusiastic ones.
In the previous chapter we have seen that, even at its most effective, Peper
Harow's struggle to function therapeutically was an uphill task in the face
of the extreme psychological injury and emotional starvation that so many
youngsters had endured. Perhaps there can be no way for this ever to be
completely overcome. However, understanding of our unconscious functioning and pathology, and of how either develops, continues to grow.
Despite great fear of the unknown, especially the unknown in our minds,
we have seen a significant development in the understanding of psychosexual issues, for instance, thus enabling problem-specific responses to be
devised and managed. Criticism of the management of sexuality at Peper
Harow, the management of transitions – both of organisational development and of each individual's separation from such an intensive
experience – emphasises, with the benefit of hindsight, the limitations of
our understanding twenty years ago. How much better might Peper
Harow, like each of us, have been had we known what we know now?
Nevertheless, and without exception, every ex-resident participant in this
study is clearly glad that they experienced Peper Harow – warts and all!

7

METHODS

This study's main objective has been to demonstrate the psychological and functional changes that have occurred within the ex-residents since they arrived at Peper Harow. Table 1 (p. 58) shows the considerable difference between how they are now and how they were then. It would be helpful to know exactly what and how much change resulted from the ex-residents' experiences at Peper Harow.

While listening to ex-residents over the years, it became increasingly clear that their comments about Peper Harow were more than simply reminiscent. Both thoughtful criticism or spontaneous comments offered important insights into what actually influenced them and brought about change. As an exceptionally articulate group, it became clear that what they could say might also be of particular use to those who work with children and young people and to those who make social policy, for the views of the consumers of care or treatment, especially children and young people, are rarely heard when policy is being developed. It also seemed that the ex-residents' courageous personal struggles with their problems deserved representation. Some people frequently dismiss change brought about by psychotherapy, with too little acknowledgement of the patients' essential emotional investment and of the courage it costs them, or of its long-term significance. Long-term psychotherapy is no easy option for either patient or therapist, however worthwhile the outcome proves to be. Nevertheless, many critics suggest that their lack of serious interest in psychotherapy is inevitable when empirical demonstrations of cause and effect are so few. Perhaps in response to such criticism or perhaps as a result of psychotherapy's continuing development, which has made it richer in variety, it has become increasingly effective in its practice. Specific research has demonstrated this. However, resistance to evidence of this still reflects the unthinking way that we as a society deal with those whose disturbed behaviour originally emanates from their own often cruel suffering. These

127

origins are ignored, ensuring that treatment for their anti-social behaviour, along with staff training and research, will be insufficiently resourced as compared with punishment. For this reason alone, long-term outcome studies are rare. It still remains possible, therefore, to continue to deny the need for treatment on the Kafkaesque basis that there is still not enough evidence of its effectiveness!

However, the existence of a group of mature adults, all of whom had reached the usual age for raising families, all of whom had shared a similar residential therapeutic experience up to twenty-five years earlier, provided a quite unusual perspective from which the experience they had received could be evaluated.

None of the previous books and published professional papers about the objects and processes of Peper Harow have focused on the way that residents or ex-residents experienced their stay. Nevertheless, although their anecdotal descriptions of Peper Harow may alone have been enlightening, it was felt that their views could be even more persuasive if their comments were presented in a more empirical form. Perhaps criteria could be applied to measure how real the ex-residents' perceived change was.

Professor Emeritus of Social Psychology, Marie Jahoda, had been interested in Peper Harow since its inception. She had long encouraged the idea that professionally rigorous research of the Peper Harow process ought to be undertaken. Even a limited undertaking required financial support, and The Tudor Trust, which had given generously to many programmes offering treatment to disturbed children and adolescents, was keen to receive hard information about outcome, even though it had not supported research projects before. The Trust's condition was that the project would be researched rigorously rather than just descriptively.

Accordingly, it was agreed to establish a Steering Committee to oversee the project, to whom the author would report his progress on a regular basis. Academic members of The Tudor Trust would sit on this committee and Professor Jahoda also agreed to be a member. A professional interviewer experienced in psychotherapy and in residential work with adolescents, Judith Arbow, was appointed as researcher and she too joined the committee that would work with the author.

The next two tasks were to establish a randomly selected sample of participants from all those who had come to Peper Harow during the period which would be studied and, at the same time, a design for the way they would be interviewed would be developed.

The Peper Harow Foundation, after consultation with ex-residents, agreed access to registers and files so that a complete list of those who had joined the Community could be established. The random sample was drawn from this. Access to the files was provided a second time so that the reports within them, written about the ex-residents before they came to Peper Harow as well as when they were resident, could be examined for additional information.

Another major source of information was the author, who had person-ally conducted the assessment of each youngster's initial referral papers as well as their admission interview, and who had been ultimately responsi-ble for their development when he had been Peper Harow's director. Although his comments are inevitably subject to bias, it is useful to have a parallel discussion of the different issues deriving from the ex-residents' treatment in the residential context. The ex-residents could not be expected to evaluate their experience except in a personal way. Additionally, while the ex-residents' comments are valuable at face level, their value can also be enhanced if some of the less obvious significance of their remarks can be clarified. Thus the basic material of the investigation consists of the tapes and transcripts of the ex-residents' interviews, the reports on their original Peper Harow files and the commentary of the ex-director concerning this material and the objectives of the Community at that time.

THE RESEARCH SAMPLE

The selection criteria for the list of potential participants, from which the sample would be selected, was that all males who had been at Peper Harow for more than two years and all females who had been resident at Peper Harow for eighteen months prior to April 1983, when the first and founding director actually left, should be eligible. It had always been felt that the time at Peper Harow required for the process to be effective was between three and five years. Quite a few youngsters left within the first two years, usually within the first six months. These tended to be people who found the psychosocial challenge to their defences intolerable and whose resistance to the peer group prevented their participation in Community activities. Nevertheless, there were also some youngsters who tended to settle well initially, yet still insisted on leaving at what for the majority had begun to be a turning point.

Unless youngsters had found a way of identifying with Peper Harow, no matter how tenuously, it soon became evident that there was nothing to hold them there. Their disturbed impulses rapidly dominated their lives once more, to the exclusion of other influences, whether of peers or of their own family or of staff. Unfortunately, it was not clear before admis-sion which youngsters would eventually engage with the programme and which would not. Therefore, we offered places to youngsters knowing that some might well not remain long enough to receive the help they needed. On the other hand, some of the most successful members of the research sample appeared very unlikely to become so when they first arrived.

Many youngsters only seemed to flirt with commitment to change but, by the time they had been at Peper Harow for about two years, they had generally turned an emotional corner. The level of use which youngsters were able to make of the opportunities at Peper Harow thereafter varied greatly. Even those who at the time of their departure still did not appear to have done well, are now able to appreciate Peper Harow's significant long-term effect on them. Young women ex-residents were included in the sample despite their more limited experience of Peper Harow. This might well have weighed against the sample's overall level of apparent success. It should be emphasised that the sampling was calculated on a random basis.

Girls were first admitted to Peper Harow in September 1980. Very few, therefore, had been there for more than two years before the period to be studied ended. Thus, although they would not have been at Peper Harow long enough to have experienced the change within themselves which boys who had been there for more than two years had experienced, it was still felt that all the women who had been at Peper Harow for eighteen months should be included in the sample to give an acceptably representative gender balance.

The admissions during the period of the study totalled 140, of which 104 had been present for the time required to be eligible for sampling. Their names were drawn from the official registers of the period and a list in order of their admission was drawn up of the 104 eligible boys. A proposed sample was taken of one in three of these ex-resident boys and all of the available ex-resident girls. The Peper Harow Foundation then wrote to them explaining what had been proposed and asking them to let the Foundation know if they did not want to participate. The researcher then attempted to make contact with the remaining people and, where this proved impossible, the next person on the original list was approached. In other words, the list was divided into groups of three and of each group a priority of order was established. Each group of three was approached in the same order. Twenty-nine men were eventually traced, all of whom agreed to be interviewed. Of the nine women who were eligible one was untraceable, one refused to be interviewed and a third failed to arrive at either of the two previously agreed appointments, thus leaving six women. During one of the men's interviews, the tape recorder developed a fault, making transcription impossible.

Thus the final sample numbered twenty-eight men and six women. This amounted to 24 per cent of everyone admitted to Peper Harow between July 1970 and April 1983 and to 32 per cent of those who were actually eligible for the sample, according to the criteria described above.

There were three recognisable phases during the overall period being studied which the sample represents adequately. Forty per cent were admitted during the first period. This was a period of transition from Peper Harow's status as an Approved School with one kind of regime, to that of a Special School functioning as a psychotherapeutic community. The ex-residents who represent this period were admitted between 1971 and 1974 inclusively. The middle period, between 1975 and 1979 inclusively, was the most settled, although many ex-residents describe the material and physical changes which took place during this period as very disturbing. Thirty-four per cent of the sample represent this period. The final period was half the length of the other two, between 1980 and 1982 inclusively. Twenty-six per cent represent this period, at the end of which the founding director left. All participants admitted during this period were affected by this event. Only one of the sample admitted during this period left in an arranged manner; the rest were either expelled or ran off and refused to come back after the founding director's departure. Because the list of those who met the initial criteria for establishing the sample had been arranged in order of admission, inevitably all stages of the Community's development were represented. Hopefully, this strengthened the general objectivity of the ex-residents' combined statements. A proportionately greater number of the sample group derive from the shorter final period, but the effect of this may only have been to reduce the sample's overall level of understanding and appreciation of the Peper Harow treatment process, which might have caused the process to appear to be less successful. There was a considerable increase in disturbance after this final period, to which those ex-residents who were there at the time refer, but this period is beyond the attention of this study. However, the ex-residents who overlapped often seem to find it difficult to differentiate between which experiences happened when. Comparison of participants' responses between these periods has not been attempted.

THE INTERVIEW – DESIGN AND PROCESS

The study aimed to discover how well the sample of today's adults reflects Freud's view that maturity is determined by the ability to love and to work. It was necessary to decide what psychosocial aspects of each research participant's life could best demonstrate their success. At the same time, whatever psychosocial achievement was evident, it needed to be compared with what they had been like before Peper Harow. Obviously, the normal and widest meaning of loving and being loved is different for an early adolescent and for a mature adult. However, in each case, the decisive indicators would derive from the way they managed relationships that were appropriate to their chronological age. For instance, the most important people in an early adolescent's life would normally still be his or her parents and siblings. An adolescent should be able to cope with the normal stresses that are special to that relationship. Despite such normal difficulties, adolescents should still be able to offer and receive emotional nurture. It is a reasonable expectation of an adult in their thirties that they would be capable of engaging in an intimate relationship with a partner and with children. In other words, adolescents and adults should both be capable of emotional intimacy in their relationships, although their specific engagement would be different because of their different age-related capabilities and psychological objectives. In adulthood, the ability to maintain such relationships over significant time would say a great deal about what one person is able to inspire and to satisfy in another and to what extent they are sufficiently emotionally self-sustaining to be able to put a partner's or their children's interests ahead of their own.

This long-term package of psychologically self-nourishing and mutually nourishing strengths in personal relationships is not altogether dissimilar from the one that sustains the ability to work purposefully. In any work situation there will always be stresses to overcome brought about by events beyond any individual's control, such as redundancy, domestic or health problems. Work includes study on a formal vocational or academic course, or functioning as a reliable employee over time, or undertaking a long-term project such as establishing a professional studio or business. A repertoire of psychological strengths are required, such as persistence, the ability to retain motivation and the ability to set aside current gratification in the pursuit of medium- to long-term goals. The ability to function with reasonable psychosocial adeptness has a significant influence both within the family and within the workplace.

Such qualities reflect an overall ability to be aware of one's self within one's environment and an ability to see ourselves as others see us and to respond appropriately. They indicate someone who can be socially acceptable at various levels of relationship because their psychological strengths can sustain them in depth. Of course, no one remains constantly at one level of functioning in all circumstances. Some participants, such as Albert, did not at the time of the interview have a very high regard for their own psychosocial maturity but, despite the view of themselves as actually expressed in their interview, they also demonstrate a greater maturity than they sometimes appreciate when they talk unselfishly and lovingly of their children, or when they are aware and appreciative of their need to be mothered themselves by their partner. Expressing vulnerability sometimes indicates an appropriate grasp of reality rather than immaturity.

Even if what the ex-residents were to say and what could be gleaned of their childhood and early adolescence from reports did demonstrate a significant change, we still needed to see what they had to say about the part that Peper Harow played in making that change. Therefore, another part of the interview was designed to obtain their view of some identifiable areas of their life at Peper Harow. They were asked about their life before admission, which often demonstrated how significant their first impressions of Peper Harow had been. They usually remembered their initial interview in detail and it had certainly been intended to make a lasting impression on them and to engage them with the psychotherapeutic process. They were asked about their experience as part of a process of change and whether their relationships with their peers, their families and the staff had changed while they were at Peper Harow. The significance of the peer group, the formal psychotherapy groups, the educational aspects and the environment, were all specific areas of enquiry also. Each ex-resident presented a different set of views about each aspect.

It would obviously be important to ensure that their responses to such questions were genuinely theirs and were uninfluenced by the way the questions were presented. Responding to an independent interviewer, instead of the ex-director, obviously made their independence easier to reinforce. The interviewer had no knowledge either of the case papers or of the individuals before the interview.

All the research interviews took place within the first three months of 1994. The two- to three-hour session was shaped by the warm and reassuring way in which the interviewer set out to establish rapport, as one would in a psychodynamic interview. Thus the first recorded questions were comparatively unstressful and open, such as, 'How are things for you these days? . . . Tell me about your partner and children, etc.' Then, 'What can you remember now about Peper Harow?'

The next stage was more focused, addressing questions about Life before Peper Harow, the Initial Interview, the Developmental Process and the issue of Departure. The interviewee having by this time felt clear that criticism was as equally acceptable as polite and positive responses, a third stage about the details of relationships, sexuality and behaviour at Peper Harow became appropriate.

The interview drew to a close with a final invitation to the ex-resident to reflect on the ways in which Peper Harow had, or had not, made a difference to his or her current life.

MANAGING THE MATERIAL

The transcripts were also produced by the interviewer. Her organisational and administrative skills were combined with her in-depth interviewing skills to produce an exceptionally accurate representation of the ex-residents' views, which could nevertheless be checked against the original tapes. The verbatim material was not altered in transcription, of course, though some reordering for the sake of clarification was made. The interviewer ensured that reordering only occurred when this did not alter the significance of the contribution.

The researcher's final task was to study each of the Peper Harow files that had been kept when each participant had been a resident. One said that he had broken into the office at that time and had stolen his file. It turned out that this was the only file that was missing. The files included all the reports that had formed part of the initial referral to Peper Harow. These might include psychiatric, social work, psychological, teachers' reports and sometimes probation reports and even parents' reports. There was also an ongoing record of the resident's life at Peper Harow, including their gurus' observations of their development. The researcher was asked to complete a proforma that was similar to the proforma which was devised to categorise the information in the transcripts.

This proforma, which summarised the transcripts, was divided into six sections. Each section was subdivided into an early Peper Harow period and a current-life period, thus enabling a comparison to be made. The sections sought evidence under the following categories:

1 Psychic coping
2 Important and sustainable relationships
3 Ability to work
4 Psychologically sustaining memory
5 Attitude towards present relationships and future life
6 Experience at Peper Harow (divided into twenty subsections)

Each individual's views were summarised in one of three boxes as either positive, negative, or too mixed for such simple polarisation. There were spaces for page references under each categorisation which directed one to quotable supporting evidence. A further proforma that recorded the arithmetical sum of these categorised opinions enabled the sample's overall view to be expressed as a percentage. When no individual view on a particular issue was expressed, no entry was made.

RESPONSE TO THE MATERIAL

As can be imagined, the interviews produced a vast amount of material to be evaluated. But the real problem to be managed was one of interpretation. Contact with the participants reawakened their emotional response to their experience at Peper Harow. It was as though time had been turned back and aspects of life at Peper Harow that had become submerged by their later experiences were aroused once more, as though the past had become the here and now. Some transcripts express the ex-residents' anger towards the director for his failure to remain in post. They suggest that by doing so the supposedly secure, nurturing and therapeutic parts of the programme would have been maintained for them. For whatever reasons, it appears that such participants found the change of directors very difficult to accept. The way this was expressed in interview seems redolent of much earlier periods in their lives when they had felt betrayed by parents who had been unable to give them a stable background. Their attitude towards Peper Harow in the research interview, therefore, could not simply be an objective and rational one but was unavoidably and phenomenally influenced by the psychotherapeutic relationship they had once had with the ex-director, and indeed with the Community as a whole, when they had all been at Peper Harow.

Thus, some remarks are coloured with feelings that seem as powerful and as real to the individual as they had been in their childhood. For instance, some ex-residents suspected that Peper Harow 'sibling' ex-residents were more valued by the ex-director than they were. Others seem to dismiss the therapeutic significance for them of Peper Harow as a totality. They acknowledge their relationships with one or two members of staff and dismiss Peper Harow as an organic and interactive organisation. They seem to regard the presence of these staff at Peper Harow as a happy coincidence, rather than because they were parts of a therapeutic totality. Such defensive polarisation is familiar in therapeutic contexts, but for it to emerge apparently unprocessed two decades later seems to indicate some remaining pathological misperception.

The unconscious but powerful emotional activity aroused by a refocusing on their past experience also aroused feelings in the interviewer and in the author that neither had fully anticipated. The interviewer sometimes came away feeling that she should try and find a therapist for the interviewee, or a job, or counsel a partner, or meet some other acknowledged

need. Sometimes she felt menaced in some indefinable way by the interviewees' misdirected hostility.

The ex-director experienced similar feelings when reading the transcripts, in addition to a whole host of feelings that a parent might feel if
one of his children were in some desperate need that he was unable to
meet. In the therapeutic context, these kinds of feelings can be used to
understand, through their arcane if nevertheless painful message, more
about the way a youngster experiences adults and the way youngsters' parents, perhaps, may have felt about their offspring. This understanding can
be used as a tool to enable the young person's confusion about what has
gone wrong to be clarified. In psychotherapy, these processes, called trans-
ference and counter-transference, are not only familiar but are actively
used as therapeutic tools which the therapist must learn to recognise and
to manage appropriately. Transferential feelings are recognised as separate
from actuality, but ensuring objective differentiation often requires considerable professional supervision. This was increasingly available to all
Peper Harow staff as the Community developed, but in this research context the initial response to the spontaneous comments in the transcripts
had to be processed independently.

Thus, before categorising each individual's response, one's own response
had to be considered and, only after that could the individual's response be
considered at a factual level as well as at a phenomenological one.
Unfortunately, the timing of the project and the initial contact with the
ex-residents occurred as Peper Harow itself was being closed. This was
experienced as an immense personal loss to the ex-residents, as well as to
the writer, and it may well have coloured everyone's responses to what
they remembered. At least such problems were recognised as requiring
great caution. However, within the same transcript, individuals often made
completely contradictory comments about the same issue. A judgement
therefore had to be reached as to whether the sum of an individual's comments was more positive or more negative but, where these were balanced,
a third category was established in order to record it. Thus, it is to be
hoped that erroneous judgement has been limited. However, if some
errors were made, they are unlikely to have been so frequent as to have
altered the overall view represented by the sum of opinion of the whole
sample.

THE TEXT

Before any writing took place, all the participants' names and those of any
of their friends or relations mentioned in the transcripts, were disguised.

All place names, except for those in the immediate vicinity of Peper Harow, were also disguised, as were the names of any other institutions to which participants referred. References to the author by name have been expressed as an initial, 'M.' and to one of the visiting consultant psychiatrists as 'N.'.

The text begins by introducing the kind of problem which Peper Harow tried to address and how it set about doing so. It attempts to show the difference between the youngsters' behaviour, functioning and prognosis before they came to Peper Harow and how they actually function as adults now. It then attempts to discuss what elements at Peper Harow caused the changes before it examines the criticisms which the youngsters have of the process. Some of these illustrate deficiencies in the programme as it existed, but other aspects seemed to highlight the intrinsic difficulty of resolving some of the longstanding personality problems caused by early deprivation and abuse. Other kinds of problem derive from the kinds of psychodynamic treatment experiences that are resisted, and yet others from those experiences that are embraced more enthusiastically.

The different viewpoints are illustrated by quotation from the transcripts, as evidential support of the overall numerical findings. The reader is left to draw his or her own conclusions as to the significance of what was achieved at Peper Harow during the period to which this study relates.

8

SUMMARY AND
IMPLICATIONS

This study reflects Peper Harow's initial period of change from a senior boys' Approved School to a mixed therapeutic community. The biggest difference is demonstrated by the contrasting daily programmes of the two organisations within an apparently similar residential context. The first set out to impose a highly regulated programme of vocational training, education and purposeful leisure activities. The second described itself as a psychotherapeutic programme within a psychotherapeutic social environment.

The Approved School saw itself as a commonsense executor of the juvenile court's best intentions. Its task was to educate and train youngsters and to socialise them as citizens and decent parents of the future. Its success would be most clearly illustrated if their hitherto escalating offending were ended. The therapeutic community saw its residents, many of whom had committed recorded offences and many of whom had committed unknown offences but also many of whom had committed no criminal offences at all, as a group of psychologically malfunctioning adolescents. Those youngsters' inability to see themselves and the world around them realistically was the result of the way their psychosocial development had been effected by experiences in their infancy and childhood. The therapeutic task was to clarify the individual connection between cause and effect and to intervene by helping each individual to achieve the psychological development appropriate to their age. This, it was felt, was what would change their anti-social behaviour permanently. It would also allow them access to the rehabilitative and socio-educational opportunities they would need in order to complete their transition from adolescence to adulthood.

All psychotherapeutic experience has shown that the enormous changes in perception and functioning which such a programme demands cannot be achieved by simple imposition. Much of the change process itself is unconscious. To the extent that it is conscious, compulsive resistance must be replaced by hope and motivation. Such a therapeutic programme takes considerable time. In a sense, such a programme will never be complete, for as well as being rehabilitational it also encompasses every person's journey through life and everyone's struggle to match their functioning with their ideals. Yet the more we come to understand, the more we cannot fail to recognise how much always lies beyond our understanding. Nevertheless, there are still major psychosocial criteria that indicate whether our life is predominantly healthy or not, which this study has examined in terms of the changes in the ex-residents' feelings about themselves and others and about the way they function psychosocially as adults.

A delinquent undertaking woodwork training in the previous Approved School programme at Peper Harow could be carefully monitored over a year and the differences measured against a scale of improvement. The day he began he was often unable to use a hammer without bending nails or bashing thumbs. He lacked confidence and he had a very short attention span. He was soon making a nuisance of himself. After a year, he could use basic tools. Under supervision he even used expensive and potentially dangerous industrial machinery and his competence and seniority boosted his sense of wellbeing and thus improved the way he presented himself. Unfortunately, his new found self-esteem often only ran skin-deep and his functioning very rapidly fell apart once he left his familiar and restricted social setting.

When we attempt to measure change within the therapeutic setting we discover how difficult it is to be objective, for value judgements about what the youngster thinks and feels cannot be entirely avoided. Evaluation in this study is not intended to be about the quality of an individual's joinery but about the way he engages in his everyday life, which tells the observer a great deal about what he feels now compared to how he felt when he first went to Peper Harow. The way he feels dictates the way he behaves, which made the ongoing judgements by staff and peers about such things as his changing capacity for self-control, extremely important. The general emphasis of these comments at Peper Harow was concerned with the individual's changing capacity for self-management, rather than as to whether his behaviour was good or bad. Of course, as we have seen, there are limits to the negative behaviour that such a community could tolerate.

Nevertheless, this therapeutic tolerance of even bad behaviour as the acceptable base from which change to good social behaviour is eventually supposed to grow, strikes many people as utter nonsense. Yet all of us are shocked by the terrible behaviour perpetrated on innocent people which we continually read about in the press and see on television. We all want it stopped! Wanting it stopped is where the 'short, sharp shockers' and the therapists actually agree, but such empirical evidence as does exist about ways of stopping such behaviour demonstrates that the effects of punishment begin to wear off the moment it is over. The evidence which Peper Harow offers suggests that its process of changing the person and coincidentally changing their behaviour would be a far more profitable direction to explore than to increase punishment. Yet governmental authorities across the Western world seem increasingly to have set their faces against treatment in the last twenty years.

This swing in policy seems to be based upon the notion that if you hurt someone enough they will eventually decide that such a price makes hurting others not worthwhile. Unfortunately, it ignores the reality that badly behaved people do not only need to stop behaving badly, they actually have to behave appropriately as an adult instead. If they have never learned how to do this, how will punishing them for their bad behaviour equip them for living appropriately? Even the huge costs of residential treatment in institutions like Peper Harow may not be expensive compared with the punitive alternative response to anti-social behaviour. Punishment is frequently re-enacted upon families and on the general public later, for the lesson of the bully teaches only that the possession of power can dictate who is free to do as they like.

Surprisingly, in the United Kingdom at least, there has been almost no researched comparison of costs between one intervention and another. As Knapp and Robertson point out in 'The Cost of Services' (Knapp and Robertson 1989), there are many complex issues that prevent comparison being made in a useful way. Perhaps one of the most difficult problems is to compare like with like. For instance, one reason why foster home placement may appear to be cheaper than a Children's Home placement could be because youngsters in the latter group may have significantly more behavioural problems and thus need a higher level of staff input. On the other hand, the costs may not really be as different as we might have supposed. Many costs are hidden or are not known but they add significantly to supposed costs – for instance, the cost of social-work time involved in finding the placement initially and in overseeing it. This may not have been added to the actual revenue costs of the placement, or even measured in the first place. In fact, the level of breakdown in foster home placement may be telling us more about the referring agency's lack of residential resources, or about its inability to recognise how seriously disturbed youngsters in its care actually are. The cost of breakdown in placement for the number of Peper Harow ex-residents who had already received more than ten previous placements was huge in financial terms. In personal terms, the cost was devastating. As a representation of society's best care of the most injured youngsters, it was shameful.

Thus, as well as the bald comparison of actual numerical costs, there is also the issue of effectiveness. It may well be more cost-effective to spend more money in the short term if it avoids spending a huge sum for an individual's lifetime and perhaps that of his children too. In a recent film about Peper Harow that updates the lives of ex-residents who first appeared in a previous film nearly twenty-five years ago, one of them agrees that his stay was very expensive, but as well as saving his life, he reflected, 'It's saved the government millions too!' (Clay 1996).

As Knapp and Robertson say:

> How does one measure the comparative or differential effectiveness of two alternative services when the dimensions of effectiveness are far from clear, when the scaling of positions along each of these dimensions is complex, when the time lags between a care intervention and the eventual impact can be huge?
>
> (Knapp and Robertson 1989: 234)

Their question is not left in a vacuum, for they suggest that if the issue were to be addressed seriously it would become possible to balance the different individual circumstances so as to clarify the cost reality.

Currently, it is equally difficult to compare outcome between different kinds of intervention. Several ex-residents suggest that had they not gone to Peper Harow they would have become confirmed criminals. Others feel certain that they would have been long-term alcoholics, or serious drug addicts. Even more feel that they would have been dead, either directly as a result of suicide or else as the probably inadvertent consequence of a destructive lifestyle. When they repeatedly declare, 'Peper Harow saved my life!' they mean it both symbolically and literally. They have no doubt about the value of Peper Harow's outcome for them, though a small number say that they would have 'got by' even without Peper Harow. The changes recorded in the study certainly add weight to those who regard their experience at Peper Harow as indispensable to their present level of development, and this despite their own criticism of certain aspects of the programme. While comparison between their present and past lives highlights dramatic changes, it is likely that these results would have been even more dramatic if some specific comparison could have been made with other kinds of institution in which youngsters with similar problems were placed. Unfortunately, it has proved impossible within the timescale and resources of this study to find comparative results. It is believed that some studies of cost and outcome do exist, but they are unpublished and with restricted access. Even those few researched outcomes into Youth Treatment Centres, Youth Custody Institutions, Adolescent Units and Approved Schools are very few and are likely to pose the same problems for accurate comparison as Knapp and Robertson suggest impede cost comparison. The impression from personal experience, for what it is worth, is that Approved Schools, for instance, had a failure rate on their own very limited reoffending criteria of about 75 per cent. The objectives for Peper Harow implied a very different set of criteria for success (Table 1, p. 58). For those without a previous record of offences, a simple comparison of reduced offending would not apply.

An article in the journal *American Psychologist* (Tate, Dickon Reppucci and Mulvey 1995) expresses concern about the move away from treatment and rehabilitation of young offenders towards their incarceration and punishment. The authors raise the same problem of finding empirical data about outcome and cost on which to base social policy instead of on the worst impulses of supposedly popular opinion. Such collusion may lure votes, but its refusal to seek effective outcome as an alternative to mechanistic punishment can only ensure the worsening of violence and deviancy in society.

Unfortunately, Tate, Dickon Reppucci and Mulvey find that even when attempts to research reality do take place:

> Studies consistently lack adequate no-treatment, comparison-treatment, or attention-only control groups and often focus solely on the outcome of the treatment programme without examining the process of how it was implemented . . . Most studies are inadequate in their description of the characteristics of their samples, the specific nature of the treatment, the conditions under which the treatment occurred and the possible effects of the administrator of treatment. Without this information it is difficult to draw conclusions about the true potential of the tested intervention and to make comparisons across programs.
>
> (*ibid.*: 777–778)

There are obvious research problems, especially when establishing comparative groups, including the familiar problem of withholding treatment from some. Although the analysis of psychological processes has become increasingly sophisticated, it still seems very difficult to ensure a sufficiently exact match of variables between a control group and an experimental group. There is also another intangible that defies easy measurement but which influences outcome and which derives from the personal characteristics of the individual professional rather than from their professional accreditation criteria and training. Advances in applied human sciences rarely begin with theory, but with the first principles of actual recorded observation. Theory is constructed later from the observer's attempt to explain the experienced process. Although we would like ultimate and empirical certainty before committing society to one approach or another, it seems that this might not be possible. Perhaps, therefore, some risk-taking is justified, if effective ways of promoting psychological and behavioural change are to be developed.

Meanwhile, this study has attempted to fulfil the need for explanatory, descriptive criteria in order to add persuasive meaning to its results. It also argues that those results are broadly impressive, even though some details of process remain imprecise. Nevertheless, it is contended that change of exceptional proportions has occurred and if final proof of cause cannot yet be established with unarguable exactitude, the indicators are extremely strong. In forming a judgement as to which social policy approach should be taken, it might be wisest in current circumstances to base our response to deviancy on the existing evidence of what has succeeded in promoting profound and long-term change of attitude and behaviour.

For all that the results of this investigation confirm many of the anticipated outcomes, they also raise other questions. As Table 2 (Chapter 3, p. 59) demonstrates, the Peper Harow population was exceptionally disturbed, and yet the combined psychosocial elements of the programme have still enabled most of its members to change fundamentally even if, as Chapter 5 suggests, some now very successful adults still bear the marks of psychological injuries that occurred in their infancy and childhood. However, although we can speculate about the reasons why a significant number of those who also received that opportunity were unable to continue long enough to achieve the same success, more initial knowledge of the circumstances leading to their disturbed functioning could help professionals engaged with similar youngsters to devise strategies that would prevent either their being rejected, or their own tendency to reject the group. Very few researchers have investigated why many predictably high-risk children do not become delinquent and disturbed in adolescence (Farrington *et al.* 1988). It appears that there are also protective factors, as well as injurious ones, in disturbed or inadequately parenting families. Could residential workers, if they understood the nature of these factors, even find a way to enhance them or to generate them within the programme? This study has not considered to what extent, if any, protective factors within the ex-residents' families have affected their ability to make use of the help available at Peper Harow. However, staff at Peper Harow were aware of both the positive and the potentially negative significance of early experience. They continually sought ways to amplify experience of child-rearing factors that make for growth and mental health.

Farrington (1990) is clear that some disturbed behaviour, such as offending, can be predicted, while Quinton and Rutter (1988) emphasise and specify the significance of intergenerational links between the behaviour of children and that of their parents. Although they demonstrate that injurious relationships between parents and children are serious indicators of later disturbance in those children, irrespective of co-existing protective factors, the negative consequences of a psychologically depriving upbringing are not necessarily inevitable. They may be avoided by changes in other circumstances, such as improved housing and material surroundings, or social and academic success at school.

> the extent of continuity (between the generations) in personal functioning is heavily dependent on the extent of continuities in circumstances and environments . . . this does not imply that the links are merely a consequence of chance and social structure . . . The links are forged both through life-chances that are outside the control of the individuals and through the actions of the people themselves, which serve either to perpetuate adversity or to break the vicious cycle of continuing disadvantage.
>
> (Quinton and Rutter 1988)

This has considerable implications for the kind of experience that treatment programmes should address. It also supports the psychotherapeutic emphasis at Peper Harow of strengthening the youngsters' positive self-perception and personal motivation to change their functioning and behaviour. Quinton's and Rutter's findings would seem to support the view that finding a way to enable apparently ineducable children to become high educational achievers was simultaneously an essential way of breaking the predictable negative course of their future psychosocial lives. A high proportion of the ex-residents clearly state that their experience at Peper Harow has significantly influenced the parenting which they now seek to provide for their own children. Therefore, in terms of preventing predictable negative outcomes, meticulous consideration of the everyday experiences that would nurture a sense of self-esteem, for instance, is of the highest importance. How organisations and staff learn to do this and are resourced so as to ensure it, becomes a priority as a result of the research evidence. Moreover, among Quinton and Rutter's findings is the optimistic recognition that the disadvantage of early life can be altered right into adulthood. Once more, therefore, research indicates the worth of investment in changing psychosocial outlook and functioning as a potentially more effective way of dealing with disturbed and delinquent teenagers than the alternative of simply repressing their anti-social behaviour for a time.

There remains a need to sharpen the focus of research into the outcome of therapeutic programmes such as Peper Harow's. For instance, Farrington points out that the behaviour of men who were delinquent in childhood and adolescence improves in their twenties, especially if they are able to establish a close relationship (Farrington 1990). Unfortunately, by their early thirties, their functioning has declined once more as they have lacked the inner resources to sustain such relationships. In this study, there were three or four ex-Peper Harow residents in their early thirties at the time of the research interview who were having difficulties in maintaining stable relationships with partners. In most cases, they were doing well in other areas such as work, so to what extent their overall functioning is in line with the population generally and to what extent it still represents a group who cannot function properly, remains unclear. Perhaps more detailed investigation would reveal the answer, or perhaps it would only add to the questions that Chapter 5 – 'The Limitation of Insight' – poses about the extent to which early damage can ever be completely resolved.

However, a great deal of research since the period which this study considers clearly emphasises that residential treatment needs to become as sophisticated as any other form of psychotherapy, if it is truly to redirect such disturbed youngsters' predictably gloomy future. The discussion in Chapter 6 – 'The Benefit of Hindsight' – is clear that the lack of a policy about the management of sexuality at Peper Harow was a serious failure, even if it was not any more naive than in most establishments at that time. Since then it has become apparent that there are several reasons why abused children are vulnerable in residential settings – though not necessarily quantitatively more vulnerable than in any other setting. Nevertheless, protecting them from further damage should be only one aim of the essential policy that any residential programme should develop to manage all sexual issues. Zahn and Schug (1993) have shown that specific therapeutic programmes to resolve past damage from abuse are, of course, essential, but the important reminder from both Schimmer (1993) and from Keith-Lucas (1993) is that youngsters in the residential setting need real help with the development of their sexuality. Hoping that psychosexual need will all somehow resolve itself invisibly, reflects adult and societal difficulties and does nothing to prevent predictable consequences. Quinton and Rutter (1988) show how the unaddressed problems of children in residential care inevitably effect their later functioning. For instance, women who have been in care are much more likely to marry a deviant spouse, or to fail to deter unwanted pregnancy, or to cope with child-rearing and to repeat unsupportive parenting. How the youngster's predilection for repetitive or comfort-seeking or identity-reinforcing behaviour can be diverted into more effective functioning could be regarded as one of the essential tasks of any programme with adolescents. Nevertheless, as the Peper Harow experience showed, it is easier said than done.

However tenaciously society may be able to grasp the wolf by the ears, the time must come for its eventual release. As Albert suggested in his transcript, if all the wolf learns during captivity is more sophisticated criminality (and still deeper resentment) the long-term cost to society will be greater in human and even in financial terms.

At the least, a significant proportion of the potentially wasted billions of pounds spent on repression should be applied to the best research possible. We may as a society have a pathological wish not to respond realistically to deviancy, but we still retain the capacity to determine social policy according to reality and would be wiser to do so.

This book did not set out to research the issue of deviancy in society and its resolution. Its task had seemed to be rather simpler, for it only sought to discover whether what we aimed for when Peper Harow was founded had been effective, and also whether with hindsight we could learn anything from the ex-residents' experience which might have improved what we did. What seems to have been revealed is that what occurred has had a more positive outcome for the ex-residents than we might have anticipated. In trying to clarify the purpose of various aspects of the process, it may be that some exceptionally effective directions have been indicated that might be useful to others in the future. The need for an optimistic process that would give hope to the many youngsters who continue to suffer, and in turn to cause suffering, certainly remains. It would also benefit society by not endlessly increasing the prison budget appropriation.

Nevertheless, several wider issues arise from this book's specific finding that most of the ex-residents in the research sample have changed enormously in their adolescence at Peper Harow and since. If the effectiveness of treatment programmes is to be increased, made more specific for need, and described sufficiently clearly so as to enable relevant staff training to occur, all these issues call for greater empirical knowledge.

Table 2 (Chapter 3, p. 59), for instance, broadly illustrates that a high level of deviance existed in the ex-residents' group when they arrived at Peper Harow. As Estella Welldon suggested in her 1996 Foulkes Lecture, effective psychotherapy for such extremely disturbed people requires very careful assessment of the treatment of choice. Even apparently similar forms of dysfunction may only be effectively managed and treated if the appropriate differentiation is made, say, between individual and group psychotherapy. And yet improved specificity in treatment may only be a part of the individual's overall need.

We do not know, of course, which ex-residents who experienced which particular problem cited in Table 2 did best. Nor do we know for sure whether any improvement, or lack of it, derived from factors at Peper Harow or from other factors, personal or environmental, such as outcome predetermining protective factors in family or environment as suggested by Quinton and Rutter (1988) or Farrington *et al.* (1988), for instance.

However, we might suggest tentatively, that the ex-residents' abilities to overcome their problems and to change the direction of their lives, might not have been possible had their individual psychotherapeutic need not been addressed within the context of a large enough organic network of relationships that shared an understanding of therapeutic needs and objectives. It might well be that the therapeutic community provides the widest context within which a variety of incompatible dysfunctions can be managed while the individual's specific psychotherapeutic needs are met.

Over thirty years ago, Lee Robins' major longitudinal research project demonstrated how many and various were the factors affecting both the causes and processes for avoiding deviancy (Robins 1966). At the same time, Professor Robins noted how little effective treatment was actually available. Factual information, whether about cause or cure, was equally limited. There had been some major studies in earlier years though little correlated understanding had been drawn from them. Nor has research since the 1960s in Western countries had more than a limited impact on social-policy makers and legislators, despite the urgent need for social and health issues to be managed more effectively. In the same way that huge investment is needed into research into the processes that cause and prevent deviancy in society, similar investment is needed to investigate normal psychosocial development. Political/economic debates such as whether there should be financial support for the families of adolescents, or whether the money should be devoted to providing for their better formal educational development, might then be informed by understanding of the essential interactiveness of all teenage experiences for successful transition to adulthood. Simply categorising children or adolescents according to administrative convenience, and funding according political bias, is disintegrative, ineffective and wasteful. Perhaps, above all, this study suggests that the link between conscious learning and psychological unconscious processes is a critical one to forge and strengthen. Almost all the ex-residents in this study's sample illustrate this.

If only for this reason, Peper Harow's closure was a great loss. Within its organisation there have been many debates about the underlying reasons for its closure. Were the psychodynamic stresses that develop within such an organisation too great to be managed? Should an unfeeling government have recognised its experimental worth and paid off its financial shortfall so as to enable it to continue? If its effectiveness declined, was this a management issue, or a clinical one? Although many readers would want to know the answers to these and other questions, this book has deliberately avoided engaging with them. Instead, it concentrated on clarifying what was meant by residential treatment at Peper Harow, and its outcome. We had no intention of ignoring the limitations of our practice and process, but we did want to make sure that what turned out to have been worthwhile was recorded. Examining the ex-residents' experiences is deeply moving and it emphasises the grievous consequences when one generation passes its hurt and confusion on to the next. But what the lives of Peper Harow's ex-residents have demonstrated since they left the Community is that the engendering of hope within them has been psychotherapeutically powerful. Hope can halt this intergenerational cycle of injury and misunderstanding and when truly aroused, its potential for changing lives restores more than the individual.

BIBLIOGRAPHY

Ackerman, N.W. and Jahoda, M. (1950) *Anti-Semitism and Emotional Disorder*, New York: Harper & Brothers.

Baron, C. (1987) *Asylum to Anarchy*, London: Free Association Books.

Bettelheim B. (1965) *Love Is Not Enough*, New York: Macmillan.

—— (1990) 'Children of the Holocaust', in *Recollections and Reflections*, London: Thames & Hudson.

Bloom, R.B. (1993) 'When Staff Members Sexually Abuse Children in Residential Care', *Residential Treatment for Children and Youth* 11, 2: 89–106.

Bowlby, J. (1966) *Maternal Care and Mental Health*, New York: Schocken Books.

Braga, W. de C. (1993) 'Experiences With Alleged Sexual Abuse in Program: I. Case Vignettes', *Residential Treatment for Children and Youth* 11, 1: 81–98.

Bunce, M. (1994) 'Essex Child Needs Survey', unpublished research report commissioned by Essex Social Services Department.

Burn, M. (1956) *Mr. Lyward's Answer – A Successful Experiment in Education*, London: Hamish Hamilton.

Butler-Sloss, E. (1988) *Report of the Enquiry into Child Abuse in Cleveland*, London: Department of Health and Social Security.

Care of Children, The – Principles and Practice in Regulations and Guidance (1990), London: Department of Health.

Charles, G., Coleman, H. and Matheson, J. (1993) 'Staff Reactions to Young People Who Have Been Sexually Abused', *Residential Treatment for Children and Youth* 11, 2: 9–21.

Children and Young Persons Act (1969) London: Department of Health and Social Security.

Children Act, The (1989) London: Department of Health and Social Security.

Clyde, J. (1992) *The Report of the Enquiry into the Removal of Children from Orkney*, Edinburgh: Scottish Office.

Clay, C. (1996) 'Bad Boys', in L. Rees (series ed.) *Timewatch*, London: BBC Television.

Cornish, D.B. and Clarke, R.V.G. (1975) *Residential Treatment and its Effects*, London: Home Office.

Erikson, E.H. (1959) 'Identity and the Lifecycle: Selected Papers', in *Psychological Issues* (Monograph) 1, 1, New York: International Universities Press.

Farrington, D.P. (1990) 'Implications of Criminal Career Research for the Prevention of Offending', *Journal of Adolescence* 13: 93–113.

Farrington, D.P., Gallagher, B., Morley, L., St Ledger, R.J. and West, D. (1988) 'Are there any Successful Men from Crimenogenic Backgrounds?', *Psychiatry* 51: 116–130.

Freud, S. (1938) *The Psychopathology of Everyday Life*, Harmondsworth: Penguin.

Goffman, E. (1968) *Asylums*, Harmondsworth: Penguin.

Johnson, T.C. and Aoki, W.T. (1993) 'Sexual Behaviours of Latency Age, Children in Residential Treatment', *Residential Treatment for Children and Youth* 11, 1: 1–21.

Kahan, B. (1994) *Growing Up In Groups*, London: Department of Health.

Keith-Lucas, A. (1993) 'Children and Love', *Residential Treatment for Children and Youth* 11, 2: 1–8.

Kilpatrick, A. (1992) *Long-range Effects of Child and Adolescent Sexual Experiences*, Hillsdale, New Jersey: Lawrence Erlbaum Associates.

Knapp, M. and Robertson, E. (1989) 'The Cost of Services', in B. Kahan (ed.) *Child Care Research Policy and Practice*, London: Hodder & Stoughton.

Millham, S., Bullock, R. and Hosie, K. (1978) *Locking Up Children – Secure Provision within the Child Care System*, Farnborough: Saxon House.

Neill, A.S. (1968) *Summerhill*, Harmondsworth: Penguin.

Ponce, D.E. (1993) 'Erotic Countertransference Issues in a Residential Center', in G. Northrup (ed.) *The Management of Sexuality in Residential Treatment*, New York: Haworth.

Quinton, D. and Rutter, M. (1988) *Parenting Breakdown – The Making and Breaking of Intergenerational Links*, Aldershot: Avebury.

Redl, F. and Wineman, D. (1951) *Children Who Hate*, New York: Free Press.

Robins, L.N. (1966) *Deviant Children Grown Up – A Sociological and Psychiatric Study of Sociopathic Personality*, Baltimore: Williams & Wilkins.

Rose, M. (1990) *Healing Hurt Minds – The Peper Harow Experience*, London/New York: Tavistock/Routledge.

Sacks, O.W. (1989) *Seeing Voices – A Journey Into the World of the Deaf*, London: Picador.

Savalle, H. and Wagenborg, H. (1980) 'Oscillations in a Therapeutic Community', *International Journal of Therapeutic Communities* 1: 3.

Schimmer, R. (1993) 'Dangerous Development: Considerations Concerning the Governance of Sexual Behavior in Residential Treatment Centers', *Residential Treatment for Children and Youth* 11, 1: 23–35.

Tate, D., Dickon Reppucci, N. and Mulvey, E. (1995) 'Violent Juvenile Delinquents', *American Psychologist* 50, 9: 777–781.

Welldon, E. (1996) 'Let the Treatment Fit the Crime', E.H. Foulkes 1996 Annual Lecture in M. Pines (ed.) *Group Analysis*, London: Sage Publications for The Group Analytic Society (London).

Winnicott, C. (1968) 'Communicating With Children', in R. Tod (ed.) *Papers on Residential Work Vol. 2, Disturbed Children*, London: Longman Green & Co. Ltd.

Zahn, B. and Schug, S. (1993) 'The Survivors Project: A Multimodal Therapy Program for Adolescents in Residential Treatment Who Have Survived Child Sexual Abuse', *Residential Treatment for Children and Youth* 11, 2: 65–88.

INDEX

Ackerman, N.W. 36–7, 60
admission: interviews 24–8, 65, 90, 133; profiles 58–9; selection criteria 27–8
adolescence 15
Adolescent Units 1, 142
adoption 31
aggression 8
alienation 105
animals, attacks on 33, 63
Aoki, W.T. 43
Approved Schools 1, 14, 19, 84–5; daily programmes 138–9; failure rate 142; Peper Harow 15, 16, 96, 97, 131, 138
Arbow, Judith 128
Assessment Centres 62, 63, 65
authority, issues about 93

babyhood 2–3
Balliol, Edward 88
Baron, C. 94
bedroom groups 68–70, 120
bedrooms 81–2
behaviour, inappropriate 10–11, 19, 103; before Peper Harow 30–7; controlling 110–11; peer-group management 21; predicting 144; protective factors 143–4; therapeutic tolerance 139–40; understanding source of 91–2, 110–11
Bettelheim, B. 10, 104–6, 107
Bloom, R.B. 6
bonding 6

Borstals 1, 19
Bowlby, J. 5, 18
Braga, W. de C. 118
Bullock, R. 24, 29
bullying 32, 34, 97, 121
Bunce, M. 7
Burn, M. 16, 18
Butler-Sloss, E. 95

camping 21, 65–7, 74, 76–7, 109
Care of Children, The (1990) 7
change: agents of 62–89; ex-residents' perceptions 61, 141; in family relationships 47–8, 58, 61, 124–5; motivation for 19–20; resistance to 17–19, 77–9, 82, 83, 98–9; role of Peper Harow 133
Charles, G. 36, 118
children (of ex-residents) 43, 47–8, 50–2, 55–6
Children Act (1989) 6
Children who Hate 17
Children of the Holocaust 104–6
Children and Young Persons' Act (1969) 6, 8
children's homes 62, 118, 120, 123; costs 140–1; inspection 7
Clarke, R.V.G. 14
Clay, C. 141
cleaning 22, 23, 83–4, 98
Clyde, J. 95
Coleman, H. 36, 118
Communicating With Children 108
Community Meeting 9, 11, 23, 72, 84, 86, 89, 91, 93, 95, 104, 112

151